Southern GRIT

Sout

...ern GRIT

100+ Down-Home Recipes
for the Modern Cook

KELSEY BARNARD CLARK

photographs by
ANTONIS ACHILLEOS

CHRONICLE BOOKS
SAN FRANCISCO

Library of Congress Cataloging-in-Publication Data

Names: Clark, Kelsey Barnard, author. | Achilleos, Antonis, photographer.
Title: Southern grit : 100 down-home recipes for the modern cook / Kelsey Barnard Clark ; photographs by Antonis Achilleos.
Description: San Francisco : Chronicle Books, [2021]. | Includes index.
Identifiers: LCCN 2020050387 | ISBN 9781797205571 (hardcover) | ISBN 9781797205793 (ebook)
Subjects: LCSH: Cooking, American--Southern style. | Cooking--Southern States. | LCGFT: Cookbooks.
Classification: LCC TX715.2.S68 C563 2021 | DDC 641.5975--dc23 LC record available at https://lccn.loc.gov/2020050387

Manufactured in China.

Photography by Antonis Achilleos.
Food styling by Rishon Hanners.
Prop styling by Mindi Shapiro.
Design by Lizzie Vaughan.
Typesetting by Taylor Roy.
Lettering by Jamar Cave.

Aperol is a registered trademark of Davide Campari - Milano S.P.A.; Atkinson's (cornmeal) is a registered trademark of Atkinson Milling Company, Inc.; Badia is a registered trademark of Badia Spices, Inc.; Ball is a registered trademark of Ball Corporation; Bundt is a registered trademark of Northland Aluminum Products, Inc.; Carolina Gold is a registered trademark of Riviana Foods Inc.; Certo is a registered trademark of Kraft Foods Group Brands LLC; Chex cereal is a registered trademark of Gardetto S Bakery, Inc.; Cholula is a registered trademark of Spicy Liquid, LLC; Conecuh Sausage is a registered trademark of Conecuh Sausage Company, Inc.; Crystal Hot Sauce is a registered trademark of Baumer Foods, Inc.; Dixie Lily is a registered trademark of China Doll Rice and Beans, Inc.; Duke's Mayo is a registered trademark of Sauer Brands, Inc.; FedEx is a registered trademark of Federal Express Corporation; Frank's RedHot is a registered trademark of The French's Food Company LLC; Heath toffee bars are a registered trademark of The Hershey Company; Honey Bunches of Oats is a registered trademark of Post Foods, LLC; Indian Head is a registered trademark of Wilkins-Rogers, Inc.; Jack Rudy Bourbon Cocktail Cherries are a registered trademark of Jack Rudy Cocktail Company, LLC; Kahlùa is a registered trademark of The Absolut Company; KitchenAid is a registered trademark of Whirlpool Properties, Inc.; Kuhn is a registered trademark of Kuhn Rikon AG; Lakeside (cornmeal) is a registered trademark of Lakeside Mills; Life cereal is a registered trademark of The Quaker Oats Company; MacGyver is a registered trademark of Auras Unlimited Productions, Inc.; Mason jars is a registered trademark of Mason Jars Company, LLC; Morton is a registered trademark of Morton Salt, Inc.; Mrs. Meyer's is a registered trademark of The Caldrea Company; Nature's Seasons is a registered trademark of Morton Salt, Inc.; Old Bay is a registered trademark of McCormick & Company, Inc.; Samoas is a registered trademark of Ferequity Inc.; Sweet Baby Ray's is a registered trademark of Ken's Foods, Inc.; Tabasco is a registered trademark of McIlhenny Company; Tajín is a registered trademark of Industrias Tajín, S.A. de C.V.; *Top Chef* is a registered trademark of Bravo Media LLC; Topo Chico is a registered trademark of The Coca-Cola Company; Wonder is a registered trademark of Flowers Foods; Worcestershire is a registered trademark of H.J. Heinz US Brands LLC.

10 9 8 7 6 5 4 3 2

Chronicle books and gifts are available at special quantity discounts to corporations, professional associations, literacy programs, and other organizations. For details and discount information, please contact our premiums department at corporatesales@chroniclebooks.com or at 1-800-759-0190.

Chronicle Books LLC
680 Second Street
San Francisco, California 94107
www.chroniclebooks.com

DEDICATION

This book is dedicated to the
original matriarchs of my
family—Grandmother June,
Great-Grandmother Lil, and
Great-Grandmother Mildred,
"Sweetie," as well as my
grandmother-in-love, Evelyn
Runell Clark, "Mimi." You passed
down your fierce, driven spirits,
and we sense your nurturing
and tender hearts in each recipe
you left us. You each broke glass
ceilings that made it possible for
my generation to become the
modern Southern woman. Thank
you, I dedicate this book to y'all.

No. 3
POTATOES, GRAINS & PASTA
114

No. 4
SEAFOOD
134

No. 5
EGGS & POULTRY
160

No. 6
PORK & BEEF
188

No. 7
BREADS & PASTRIES
208

Introdu

uctioN

Getting Started

Hey y'all! I am thrilled to throw my doors open and welcome y'all into my little life. I am a chef, mother, wife, plant enthusiast, animal lover, thrifter, MacGyverer, and protector of tradition. I believe in the old way of doing things, but am the first to stand in line for progress and change. I cook the way your grandmother would and am an advocate for a traditional kitchen. I was raised to believe you catch more flies with honey, but I often have the temperament and brashness of a true New Yorker. I was the first to leave home, saying I would never return, and the first to come back. I am a proud Southern woman and aim to make things better than the way I found them.

There's nothing quite like being raised Southern. There's a certain way we keep our house, fix our food, draw out our words, and know how to do a little bit of everything. We're frugal yet giving and have mastered the art of throwing a damn good party. We love big, and we send our thank-yous on stationary. We require a "yes ma'am" and "no sir" from our children and love them in a monogram. We know the importance of planning ahead, preparation, and putting up a summer's crop. We are never in a hurry, with time moving as slow as sugarcane syrup, but we are always prompt.

The South is the place I ran from and then returned to. The place I decided to settle down, buy a house, raise a family, and build a business. It's the place I called home and now, the home I've chosen. The South that has shaped me is what I want to share with you.

First things first: Preparation is key. Southerners haven't been putting up fruits and vegetables for generations for nothing! A little forethought will save you buckets of time. The term *mise en place* ("everything in its place") is widely used in professional kitchens. It's all you need to say to someone in a kitchen for him or her to know exactly what you are talking about. "Do you have your MEP ready?" "Have you mise'd out that recipe yet?" "Does the front of house have their MEP for service?" It also happens to be my mantra for life and one of the most important lessons before we get to cookin'. This term was drilled into us throughout culinary school and then in professional kitchens, but it wasn't until I returned home to the South that I realized why this idea wasn't new to me. You see, we are born and bred to be prepared in the South. Hunters are first taught how to prepare and safely operate a gun before they ever shoot off a round. We learn to organize a toolbox properly, disassemble and master every knot before we ever catch a fish on a reel. Our cans are cleaned, sterilized, and lined up in a straight line before we ever fill them with jam. Southerners have mastered the art of being prepared. We take the time to teach, and we're never in a hurry when doing so. Simply put, we have our shit together.

This may be hard to hear, but to *appear* to have your shit together, you've actually got to *have* it together. I know, I know. "But I have a newborn!" "But I have a toddler!" "But I work all the time!" I get it. But I swear you'll thank me for this. Because chances are you picked up this book because you want to know how I "do it all." How I tend the garden, keep houseplants alive, and put an edible meal on the table by 7 p.m. How I keep the floors clean, the toilets white, and a restaurant operating seven days a week. Sometimes shortcuts are the fastest way

to your destination, and I am all about sharing my best-kept detours. I'll be the first to admit my mistakes, tell you all about my worst ideas ever, and help y'all learn from my trials and errors. This is the thing: It doesn't have to be perfect—it just has to be done.

We're focusing on real-life solutions for those real-life time constraints. Good news: I happen to be one of those real people too, and guess what?! NOT PERFECT OVER HERE, Y'ALL. So let's get your house mise'd out so we can get to the fun stuff—like biscuits. Everyone loves biscuits. And cinnamon rolls and gumbo and basically everything that requires at least one entire stick of butter.

Find your happy spot, pop a bottle of bubbles—it better be a brut—and let's get started. We've got a lot of ground to cover, y'all.

THE WELL-STOCKED SOUTHERN PANTRY

We Southerners can't cook a meal without a few staples. Depending on where you live, you may need to source some of these ingredients ahead of time.

BACON

When I was living in New York, a friend asked me if there was anything we Southerners didn't put bacon in. I told him yes, but then we use sausage. Thick sliced, applewood smoked is my favorite.

BACON FAT

Every time I cook bacon (as well as chicken, FYI) I reserve the fat and keep it in a Ball jar in the fridge. It will keep for up to 6 months and will be a game changer in some of these recipes.

BUTTERMILK

You'll see this tangy cream in a lot of my recipes. If you forget to pick it up at the store, substitute by adding 1 Tbsp of white vinegar to 2 cups [480 ml] of milk. It will curdle like the real stuff.

CONECUH SAUSAGE

This Alabama-made product is my favorite. In my house we eat it at breakfast, lunch, and dinner. It's not greasy and has a balanced smoky and spicy flavor. We buy it in bulk and keep it in the freezer. If you can't source it, I suggest asking for a smoky, slightly spicy sausage, tasting and finding the one you love.

CORNMEAL

When I competed on *Top Chef*, we were allowed to bring twelve of our own ingredients in a "chef bin." My chef bin for the finale had five bags of different types of cornmeal. While you don't need all five, I do recommend you keep both white and yellow cornmeal on hand, as they cook completely differently and are used for different applications. Some of my favorites are Dixie Lily, Indian Head, Lakeside, Abbitt's, and Atkinson's.

CREOLE SEASONING

I can't think of anything that doesn't taste better with a dash of Old Bay.

DUKE'S MAYONNAISE

This is the official mayonnaise of the South. If I'm not making my own (and let's face it, with a restaurant and two young children at home, I am not), this is what I use every time. Mayonnaise is the main ingredient in the Cheat Sauces that serve as the finishing touch to many of my recipes and make you look like you've whipped up something fancy, so might as well grab two jars! If you can't get your hands on this Southern favorite, no worries—just find your favorite high-quality mayonnaise and sub it out for that.

FIELD PEAS

By field peas I mean lady peas, lima beans, butter beans, and black-eyed peas. Down South, it's an ordeal and often an entire summer day spent "putting up peas" where we blanch, clean, bag, and label them to freeze for the winter. I keep at least four bags in the freezer. Whether you put them up yourself or buy them already frozen, just be sure you have some on hand. They're the best quick side dish or add-in to salads.

FRESH HERBS

There are fresh herbs aplenty at the store, but I highly recommend growing your own. They will always be fresh; they will green up your kitchen, windowsill, or yard; you'll save money; and you'll be able to add brightness and flavor to any dish without having to leave your house. Win, win, win.

GRITS

By grits I mean stone ground yellow grits. I never mean quick grits.

HAM HOCK

I keep hocks in my freezer. I use them in everything from soups to collards. Their smokiness is like no other.

HOT SAUCE

My go-to Southern brands are Crystal and Tabasco. They both have the right balance of heat and vinegar.

KOSHER SALT

Throw out that iodized stuff, get rid of that shaker, and buy a grinder if you want a finer salt for the table. Unless I indicate otherwise, when a recipe calls for salt, I mean coarse ground kosher salt.

OLIVE OIL FOR COOKING AND FINISHING

I primarily cook with an average store-bought extra-virgin olive oil. It's also good to stock a nice olive oil—specifically Italian imported—for finishing dishes.

ONIONS

Unless I indicate otherwise, when a recipe calls for onions, I mean white or yellow.

PEELED GARLIC

PSA: It's just as fresh as an unpeeled head of garlic. I have literal nightmares from my time at Café Boulud where, as a rite of passage, I had to peel garlic for hours on end in the basement. I smelled like a big old bulb of garlic for a solid 6 months.

PURE HONEY

There is a big difference between pure honey and your average store-bought kind. Many store-bought honeys are cut with corn syrup, which cuts the flavor and the health benefits. Find a local honey source and stock up. We add ours to our coffee every morning, and our son drizzles it on his waffles in lieu of syrup.

SORGHUM SYRUP

If molasses and honey had a baby, it would be sorghum. It's sweet and flavorful without being maple or floral.

SWEET BARBECUE SAUCE

I make my own, but I also keep a few store-bought bottles in the pantry for when I'm in a pinch. Sweet Baby Ray's is a Southern staple and personal favorite.

SWEET POTATOES

We put them in pie, dot them with marshmallows at Thanksgiving, and roast them whole for our babies. They are one of my favorite daily sweet treats, and they are packed with nutrients.

UNSALTED BUTTER

There will never, ever be a day when I call for salted butter. Using unsalted allows you to control the amount of salt in the final product, and I'm a control freak, OK?

VINEGARS AND ACIDS

I always have apple cider, rice wine, red wine, and balsamic vinegar stocked, and I keep a drawer full of lemons and limes. More often than not, the "just something missing" of any dish is a splash of acid to brighten it up.

CHEF'S TOOLS

When it comes to cooking gadgets and tools, I like to keep it simple. Knowing how to use the basics well will take you just as far as having all the fanciest cooking contraptions. Here are the essentials that you just can't—and shouldn't—cook without.

BENCH SCRAPER

I prefer a metal one—it's the best way to clean up flour and dough. No more making glue with a sponge.

BUTCHER'S TWINE

You can't make the most perfect roast chicken of your life without it.

CAST IRON SKILLET

I primarily cook in cast iron. You don't need five, just one medium, well-seasoned skillet. I find the best ones at local flea markets.

FISH SPATULA

This one is tricky because the name is deceptive. Want to know what else you can use a fish spatula for? Literally everything. I mean, listen, it is the best thing to get a seared fillet out of the pan, but this little guy has so much more potential. It has a sharp, knife-like edge, so it can be used for anything

where you need a razor-thin scrape. Removing brownies from a pan, serving pie, cutting lasagna? Behold the fish spatula.

FOOD PROCESSOR

There is nothing that can purée, mix, and blend like this sucker. I use mine for just about everything—chopping mirepoix for soup; making salsas, jams, and sauces; the list goes on and on. She's my sidekick, my bestie for the restie in the kitchen.

KITCHENAID STAND MIXER

Listen, I've heard people say they prefer mixing by hand, their grandma always used a handheld mixer, yada yada. The reality is that you won't go into a professional kitchen and not see a KitchenAid stand mixer. Just get one—you need it, and your elbow will thank you.

KNIVES

There is misconception in the home cooking world that you need a big fancy knife set. Really, you just need one good 8 to 10 in [20 to 25 cm] chef's knife, plus a paring knife and a serrated knife. Learn how to sharpen your chef's knife, and keep it sharp.

MANDOLINE

Another chef must-have. Do you ever see those paper-thin cuts and wonder how we do it so consistently? Meet the mandoline, y'all.

MIXING BOWLS

Small, medium, and large, stainless steel only. Glass is too heavy to work with and nearly impossible for tossing salads or pasta.

OYSTER SHUCKER

Look for one with a wood handle and sharp tip.

PARCHMENT PAPER

Wax paper is not a substitute. Foil is also not a substitute. OK? Bonus points if you can get the precut sheets that fit perfectly on your sheet trays. Time-saver hack.

ROUND RING MOLD SET

These come in a little tin with about ten different sizes. I use them for biscuits, cheese straw crackers, and more. They're handy, trust me.

RUBBER SPATULAS

You cannot properly scrape the sides of a mixing bowl without these. You cannot properly bake without properly scraping the sides of said mixing bowl. Moving on.

STURDY, THICK SHEET PANS

For the love of all things holy, please throw away your entire collection of flimsy, dented cookie sheets, and all the nonstick coated ones, too. I beg you. Purge, get the good ones, and be floored when all of your cookies miraculously bake evenly!

TONGS

The best tool when the food's too hot to use your hands.

VEGETABLE PEELER

Every chef keeps a sharp, pro-quality peeler in their knife kit. I swear by Kuhn; it's as sharp as a razor, and it costs less than ten dollars.

WHISK

Just to be clear, I mean a good whisk. I get that y'all probably have one at home, but can you get your mashed potatoes smooth without a single loop popping out? If the answer is no, it's time to upgrade.

WOODEN AND METAL SPOONS

Plastic spoons are where good cooking goes to die. They are flimsy and can't withstand heavy stirring or beating. Wooden and metal. Do not make me say this again.

29

KNIFE SKILLS

························

I refer to a number of different knife cuts throughout the book. I'm not expecting y'all to turn into pros overnight, but listen up: Size matters. Some recipes can change drastically by using the wrong cut. Here is an illustration so you can be sure to get the right size for the recipe.

MINCE

CHOP

BRUNOISE

BATONNET

SMALL DICE

MEDIUM DICE

LARGE DICE

JULIENNE

ROUGH CHOP

CHIFFONADE

CANNING 101

Canning is a way of life in the South. Having homemade salsa, jam, and pickles in the pantry gives me a sense of well-being; eating them is a delicious reminder of seasons past. Here is the step-by-step to master old-fashioned canning.

MATERIALS

- ➤ Glass preserving jars with two-piece lids (I use Mason or Ball)

- ➤ Two hot water canners or two deep, wide Dutch ovens with a lid and rack

- ➤ Ladle or measuring cup with handle

- ➤ Tongs, jar lifter, or thick rubber garden gloves (my personal favorite)

- ➤ Funnel

- ➤ Lots of kitchen towels

CANNING STEPS

No. 1

Check Equipment

If you don't have a canning pot that includes a water-bath canner with a rack, I highly recommend purchasing one before you attempt any canning recipes. In this case, "making do" and attempting without the necessary equipment can be more than just a big pain—honestly, it can be dangerous.

No. 2

Sterilize

Y'all know I love tradition, but sometimes it's best to take advantage of the modern amenities we've been given. For hot-water canning, I'm a huge fan of the dishwasher. Load the jars and lids into the empty dishwasher, run on quick cycle or sanitize, and keep the jars hot until you fill them (that is, don't open the door). If the jars cool off before the hot food is poured in, they'll crack.

No. 3

Fill and Process

Fill the canning pot with the rack halfway with water and bring to a simmer over medium-high heat. Cover the pot and keep the water simmering while you fill the jars. Remove the jars from the dishwasher and, using a funnel or sterilized ladle, fill the jars with whatever you're canning, leaving ½ to 1 in [12 mm to 2.5 cm] of space from the rim. Be sure the food you're pouring into the jars is hot. Wipe the rim of each jar with a clean, damp towel and then screw on the lid as tightly as possible. Using tongs or wearing heavy-duty gloves, place the sealed jars on the rack in the pot, about 1 in [2.5 cm] apart. The water should come up 1 to 2 in [2.5 to 5 cm] on the sides of the jars, but no higher. Cover the pot and bring to a rolling boil. Let boil for 15 minutes.

No. 4

Cool and Store

Turn off the heat and uncover the pot. Let the jars rest for 5 minutes to cool slightly. Lay out kitchen towels in a place where the jars can sit undisturbed overnight. Remove the jars and place them upright on the kitchen towels, leaving a 1 in [2.5 cm] space between jars. Cool the jars for 12 to 16 hours. After 12 to 16 hours, check the seal by pressing on the lids. If a lid does not move and feels firm, it is sealed. If a lid moves up and down, it is not sealed. Refrigerate any jar that is not sealed and consume its contents within 1 week. Store the sealed jars in a cool, dark place for up to 12 months.

BASIC COOKING VOCAB

BAKE

When I bake something in the oven, I am always referring to convection bake. Using convection circulates the heat throughout the oven, leading to a more efficient, even bake. If you don't have a convection oven, no worries; just be careful when placing items directly on the top or bottom of the oven, as these are the hottest spots. And please listen to me when I say this loud and clear: I do not believe you need to use different oven temperatures or baking times for convection or standard baking. This is a myth, y'all.

BROIL

I often broil large items that I want to brown on one side but can't sear in a pan, such as a large roast or whole chicken. Broiling cooks the top of food at high heat, creating a "sear" effect.

NAPPE

This term refers to a consistency that will thinly, evenly coat the back of a spoon; from the French *nappe* ("tablecloth"). I use this to refer to the consistency of a sauce or jam when it is finished.

POACH VERSUS BRAISE

Both terms refer to cooking something in liquid. When braising, you typically sear the ingredient first, then cook for a long period of time. Poaching is used for more fragile ingredients that cannot be browned over high heat first; ingredients are cooked for a shorter period of time overall.

ROLLING BOIL

This is an aggressive boil where your water looks like waves coming to shore.

SEAR

Searing cooks something on super-high heat, almost to the point where your pan is smoking.

SIMMER

Simmering water is hot and steaming but with very little movement—that is, slightly bubbling in one or two spots.

KEEPING CLEAN WITH (OR WITHOUT) TODDLERS

There are a few things I swear by to keep your house clean—even with little ones around. Making small moves all day prevents tasks from becoming daunting. Tiny handprints on the fridge are the only mess I like to see. They get higher every week, and I dread the day they'll be gone.

KBC COMMANDMENTS FOR A CLEAN, CALM HOME

➤ **Clothes shouldn't touch the floor.** Dirty goes in the hamper, clean gets hung up immediately. Exceptions can be made for afternoon delights and champagne nights.

➤ **Do a load of laundry every day or every other day.** I rotate—babies', ours, towels, sheets, miscellaneous. Pro tip: Have your children strip off their school clothes when they walk in the door and immediately place them in a soak bucket. No more scrubbing stains!

➤ **Make up your bed every single day.** Trust me, you'll feel better. Pro tip: Keep a throw quilt over your nice duvet. Let the dogs lie, kids jump, and coffee spill. When your guests show up, pull that ole thing off to reveal your miraculously pristine bed.

➤ **Never let a dish sit in the sink.** I was raised on the practice of cleaning the dish right after I ate. We hardly ever used our dishwasher, and I don't to this day. But if you do use your dishwasher—no judgment here—load it as you cook and run it once it's full. Remember, it doesn't matter how you clean it, just get it done.

➤ **Tuck your house in before you go to bed.** I'm not talkin' about pulling out your broom and mop. But do make yourself a clean (or at least tidy) slate to wake up to. Clear off the counters. Put all the dishes in the dishwasher. Pick up the toys. Fold that last load of clean laundry. Don't put off for tomorrow what can be done today—chances are it won't happen, and that's how piles begin.

➤ **Kids should eat sitting down at a table—with silverware and a plate.** That's all I'm gonna say about that.

- **Wipe down your counters and burners after every meal or every cook.** I can learn just about everything I need to know about a person by looking at their stove. To do the job, I love Mrs. Meyer's Lavender All-Purpose Spray.

- **Sweep one room plus your kitchen every day.** Mop once a week and spot wipe daily.

- **Remember my life motto, mise en place?** I swear it's appropriate for all the things, all the time. I keep bins on hand to put in the pantry, drawers, fridge, and other storage spots. My junk drawer is organized by cords, lip balms and lotions, and so on. You'll be amazed at how much calmer your life feels when you have a place for everything and everything in its place.

- **Realistic expectations.** If you cohabitate with someone, have a convo with them about expectations and responsibilities—preferably before you move in. Keep up your end of the bargain, and hopefully they will as well. My husband and I are far from perfect, but we do a damn good job at maintaining our house, and we don't argue about tasks. It's because we had that convo early on and have been true to it. For example, I cook and he cleans. I water indoor plants and he handles outdoor. I do all the laundry and will not touch a diaper pail bag. Unspoken assumptions accomplish only one thing—making an ass of you and me.

HOSTESS WITH THE MOSTESS

I may have more of a passion for throwing a party than I do for cooking (gasp!). I am a junkie for a theme party. While I was pregnant with my first child, I'd get asked, "Are you nervous about the birth?" Or "What are you doing about childcare?" People always remarked how eerily calm I was about all the big stuff. The reality was, all I could think about was how big his baptism party would be and what the invitations would look like.

KBC COMMANDMENTS FOR A HOSTESS-READY HOUSE

➤ **Everyone loves a good cocktail napkin.** Every Southern woman loves a monogrammed one. There's a saying in the South that "if it ain't movin'—monogram it." In my house, even my dogs' collars and children's shirts are monogrammed, so . . . I keep holiday cocktail napkins in labeled ziplock bags and have a bag specifically for monogrammed napkins for those off-season get-togethers (I'm talkin' to you, January and September).

➤ **Keep the diffuser running and scented candles on hand.** A house feels cleaner when it smells nice, and there's just something inviting about a flickering candle. Also—toddlers are smelly, and so are dogs. Ain't no shame in hidin' it.

➤ **Always have sparkling water or sparkling mineral water in the fridge for your nondrinkers or pregnant friends.** Champagne for everyone else, duh. If they don't like either, then why did you let this crazy person into your home?

➤ **Always have ingredients on hand to throw together a charcuterie board last minute.** Keep an array of the following on hand at all times: cheese, olives, pickles, pepper jelly, pimiento cheese, good crackers, nuts, cheese straws (they keep in the freezer forever). This is why having pickled things around is key (they keep forever). And if it all goes to hell in a handbasket, pop some corn and dump it into cute bowls. If your guest doesn't like popcorn, then why did you let this crazy person into your home?

- **For the love of green, get some plants.** They create an inviting, relaxed atmosphere—plus they're good for the air in your house. I'm not saying you have to have a full-blown greenhouse like I do (it's a problem I'm not willing to admit), but even you brown-thumbers can keep a snake plant alive.

- **Even if you don't have children, if you have friends with children, try to keep a few juice boxes and kid-friendly snacks around.** It's beneficial for everyone when children are fed and entertained. Whiny, hungry kids are the worst!

- **Buy a record player and invite guests to pick a record.** Ella Fitzgerald, Johnny Cash, James Taylor, and Van Morrison never disappoint. Bonus points? Make it a drinking game.

- **Collect soft throws in pretty patterns.** Keep them in baskets for guests to grab if it's chilly. They are also great to throw on that old couch with the stain you can't get out.

- **Always prep food for more than you expect.** Add two if you're planning on ten, five if you're planning on twenty. I'm not much of a bettin' person, but odds are it'll get eaten.

- **If you're planning to host outside, also plan to *not* host outside.** It pains me to watch people frantically setting up their furniture, cleaning the living room, and moving things this and there when the skies decide to open up. Have your backup room ready to go in the event that you've gotta change your plans. Worst-case scenario, your room is spotless to enjoy after the party.

GREEN THUMB

I have an unabashed affinity for all things green. My wedding bands are emeralds, and I have more plants in my house than towels. There's a scene in The Great Gatsby *where Gatsby is getting Nick Carraway's house prepared for his oh-so-anticipated meeting with Daisy. The house is covered floor to ceiling with orchids. On my twenty-ninth birthday, my husband gifted me twenty-nine orchids. Some may say this is over the top; I say it's just right.*

In short, plants make people happy. I have no scientific data—they just do. I mean—they give us oxygen, y'all!

Your house will feel cleaner with a few vases of clippings, and there's no better quick fix to make a room feel fresh. Place them in the locations you know people will see—kitchen, powder room, entryway. When you're having houseguests, a flower on a nightstand or branch in a vase can make them instantly feel welcome.

47

FIVE WAYS TO GREEN YOURSELF

№. 1

Water

Water your plants once a week on the same day. I water all of my indoor plants on Tuesday afternoon. I've hardly ever killed a plant. Errrrrrrone loves a good routine.

№. 2

Mayo

Want to know the trick to makin' those leaves shine? Mayo, y'all. Put on a glove and wipe the leaves down. They'll love you for it—they told me so. Also, your dogs may love it. Double clean if you ask me.

№. 3

Forage

Don't break the bank, y'all. I keep a pair of clipping shears in my cars and on my stroller, and I clip out of my neighborhood 75 percent of the time. Vacant houses, "middle ground" yards, and for-rent office buildings are my jam. Basically, forage wherever you can find freebies in your neck of the woods. I've never been yelled at (yet). My faves: magnolia branches and cotton for fall; camellias, paperwhites, and Japanese magnolia for winter; cherry blossoms, tulips, and lilies in spring; and hydrangeas and everything in the summer.

№. 4

Go Easy

If you're one of those who just cannot keep a plant alive, then don't buy fiddle-leaf figs, maidenhair ferns, or orchids, 'K? Let's not go and set ourselves up for failure right off the bat. But hey, there's some good news: Do buy snake plants, zz plants, and pothos plants. If you kill these, then stay away from animals too. Just kidding. But not really.

№. 5

Thrift

Start visiting your local thrift/antique stores, and find a vintage pattern to fall in love with. I became obsessed with blue and white chinoiserie years ago and have loved collecting it over the years. Use unique pieces as planters. It doesn't have to be a pot to work like one! While you're at it, pull out your grandmother's silver, and enjoy your nice jewelry too; I do! Displaying and using sentimental pieces will inspire you to keep everything else up too.

Happy Bites

Hour & Sips

Classic Boiled Peanuts

2 TO 5 SERVINGS

I live in the peanut capital of the world. Literally: It's our town slogan. We grow, sell, shuck, roast, boil, bake, and talk peanuts. When you're "famous" here, you get a life-size peanut replica of yourself to proudly display in front of your business. A *Top Chef* peanut wearing a green apron, high ponytail, and knife roll sits in the courtyard of KBC. She's holding a tray of oysters in one hand and a glass of champagne in the other. She's more popular for fan photos than I am. Small towns do weird things.

In this part of Alabama, you can't drive more than ten miles without seeing a "Hot Boiled Peanuts" sign on a roadside produce stand. When I was growing up, the "Boiled Peanut Man" on the corner of Ross Clark Circle and Main Street had claim to the best green peanuts you've ever put in your mouth. They were delicious, no doubt, but I believe that his reputation and sunny demeanor far outshone his famous peanuts. Mr. Trawick always wore overalls, a farmer's hat, and glasses. He was the wise, patient, story-telling grandpa to everyone. He sat in the same spot, rain or shine, scooping out peanuts with a big, friendly smile. He's no longer here to pass out his giant cups of famous peanuts, but a life-size peanut replica sits right where he perched for over thirty years. Every time I catch a glimpse of that hat in the rearview mirror, I'm reminded to slow it down and pay it forward.

2 lb [900 g] fresh, green peanuts (if you can't find fresh, do not substitute)

½ cup [120 g] salt

Place the peanuts and salt in a large stockpot with 2½ qt [2.4 L] of water and bring to a boil. Lower the heat, cover, and let simmer for 8 to 10 hours, or until the peanuts are tender. Taste and add more salt if needed. Place the entire pot with the liquid in the refrigerator to cool completely. Reheat and drain to serve warm, or simply drain to serve cold. The peanutes will keep refrigerated in an airtight container for up to 1 week.

VARIATION   Cajun Boiled Peanuts

If you prefer a spicier version, add 2 jalapeño peppers, sliced into strips; 2 banana peppers, sliced into strips; 2 Tbsp of red pepper flakes; 1 Tbsp of Old Bay seasoning; and 1 tsp of black peppercorns to the peanuts and water before boiling. Then cook as directed.

➤ NOTE ◄

I like to cook my peanuts the morning before I want to eat them. I let them simmer all day, then refrigerate them in their liquid overnight. The next day, I warm them back up or eat them cold. The process of cooking and then cooling allows the carbs to turn to sugar, enhancing the peanuts' natural sweetness and intensifying the flavors.

Mama's Pantry Plate

I created this snack board for the supper menu at KBC. It started as a Southern spin-off of a classic charcuterie board. I wanted it to feel like a plate your grandmother would throw together last minute when you visited her on a Sunday afternoon. A no-fuss dose of Southern comfort. Pickles and pepper jelly put up last summer, bacon still sitting on the counter from breakfast, cheese straws from the stash in the freezer, and pimiento cheese whipped up for your visit. And so, Mama's Pantry Plate was born.

In addition to the Southern staples that anchor this plate, I encourage you to add what you like—it's supposed to be thrown together with whatever you have in the pantry. Some of my favorite accompaniments are bacon, ham, sausage, grapes, dried fruits, olives, pickles, nuts, wasabi peas, jam, Dijon mustard, crackers, and pretzels. You can't go wrong!

······ **NOTE** ······

At home, each summer I put up jars of pickled okra from my garden. At the restaurant, I use store-bought. Whichever route you go, these are divine. The acid in the pickled okra perks up this classic Southern side dish. They are especially delicious when dipped in Cheat Sauces (page 104).

Fried Pickled Okra
—— **4 TO 6 SERVINGS**

1 cup [125 g] all-purpose flour

½ cup [65 g] fine ground white cornmeal

1 tsp onion powder

1 tsp garlic powder

1 tsp freshly ground black pepper

½ tsp salt

¼ tsp cayenne

½ cup [120 ml] buttermilk

1 Tbsp hot sauce, preferably Crystal

5 cups [1.2 L] canola oil for frying

Two 16 oz [450 g] jars pickled okra

In a medium bowl, combine the flour, cornmeal, onion and garlic powders, pepper, ¼ tsp of the salt, and the cayenne and set aside. In a separate medium bowl, whisk together the buttermilk and hot sauce.

In a large skillet or Dutch oven, heat the oil to 350°F [175°C].

Toss the okra in the buttermilk mixture to evenly coat, then dredge in the cornmeal mixture. Using a slotted spoon and working in batches to avoid overcrowding, place the battered okra in the oil and fry for 2 minutes, until golden brown. Remove with a slotted spoon and place on a plate lined with paper towels to drain the excess oil. Sprinkle the okra with the remaining salt and enjoy immediately.

cont'd

Cheese "Straw" Crackers
—— 4 TO 6 SERVINGS

1 lb [450 g] extra-sharp Cheddar cheese, grated cold then brought to room temperature

½ cup [115 g] unsalted butter, at room temperature, plus more for greasing the sheet pan

2 cups [250 g] all-purpose flour

1 tsp salt

¼ tsp Old Bay seasoning

⅛ tsp white pepper

Preheat the oven to 325°F [165°C]. In a stand mixer with the paddle attachment, beat the cheese and butter together on medium to high speed for 15 to 20 minutes, until the mixture reaches the consistency of thick whipped cream. In a separate bowl, combine the flour, salt, Old Bay seasoning, and white pepper.

Gradually add the flour mixture to the cheese mixture in large spoonfuls, beating well after each addition until completely incorporated.

Grease a sheet pan and line it with parchment paper. Roll out the dough on a floured surface until it is about ¼ in [6 mm] thick. Using a 1½ to 2 in [4 to 5 cm] round ring mold, punch out circles. Place ½ in [12 mm] apart on the prepared sheet. Bake for 6 to 10 minutes or until light golden. Enjoy immediately, or cool and place in an airtight container or sealed bag in the pantry for up to 2 days.

Pepper Jelly
—— THREE 1 PT [480 ML] JARS

6 cups [1.2 kg] sugar

1½ cups [360 ml] apple cider vinegar

½ cup [90 g] minced red bell pepper

¼ cup [35 g] minced banana pepper

¼ cup [35 g] minced jalapeño pepper

½ cup [65 g] pectin (I like Certo best)

In a saucepan over medium-high heat, combine the sugar, vinegar, and peppers and bring to a rolling boil. Remove from the heat and whisk in the pectin. To store, see Canning 101 (page 34).

◼ NOTE ◼

This cheese "straw" is rolled and punched out like a dough rather than piped in strips. The cracker shape holds garnishes like a little boat. Don't have a ring mold to stamp out crackers? Use the edge of a drinking glass to create the same effect. If you want to create a classic cheese straw, simply use this recipe but press the dough through a cookie press to create 1 in [2.5 cm] long straws. Bake for 10 to 12 minutes, or until golden and crispy.

Black-Eyed Pea Hummus
—— 4 TO 6 SERVINGS OR 3 CUPS [720 G]

One 15.8 oz [445 g] can black-eyed peas, rinsed and drained

¼ cup [60 g] tahini

3 Tbsp fresh lemon juice

2 garlic cloves

¾ tsp fine sea salt

½ tsp cumin

2 Tbsp extra virgin olive oil

In a food processor, combine the black-eyed peas, tahini, lemon juice, garlic, salt, and cumin. Process briefly and then, with the processor running, alternate adding the olive oil and 2 to 4 Tbsp of water in a slow, steady stream. Purée for 3 to 5 minutes, or until completely smooth and creamy. Serve chilled or at room temperature. The hummus will keep refrigerated in an airtight container for up to 1 week.

Pimiento Cheese
—— 4 TO 6 SERVINGS OR 2 CUPS [200 G]

1 cup [100 g] freshly grated extra-sharp Cheddar cheese

⅓ cup [35 g] freshly grated smoked Gouda

½ cup [90 g] jarred pimiento peppers

¼ cup [60 g] sour cream

¼ cup [60 g] mayonnaise

½ tsp Old Bay seasoning

¼ tsp smoked paprika

Salt

Freshly ground black pepper

In a mixing bowl, stir together the Cheddar, Gouda, pimientos, sour cream, mayonnaise, Old Bay seasoning, and smoked paprika with a wooden spoon until completely incorporated. Season with salt and pepper. Serve chilled or at room temperature. The mixture will keep refrigerated in an airtight container for up to 1 week.

✦ NOTE ✦

I always use freshly grated cheese. Preshredded cheese is coated with cellulose to prevent clumping, which can be helpful but lacks the flavor and creaminess of fresh grated. It also fails to melt properly and tends to dry out faster.

Chicken Liver Pâté and Fig Jam

8 TO 10 SERVINGS

I learned how to make pâté working at Café Boulud in NYC. We used foie gras and a layer of fig jelly as clear as glass. Preparing this dish was when I started to connect French and Southern cooking and see a web of tradition that often intertwined. It sparked my passion for creating Southern notes in every dish I make and began my obsessive study of the history of Southern cooking—not just the European influences but also the African and Native American roots that are so often unsung in fine dining restaurants, as well as the general make-do-with-what-you-have ethos.

Today I make my pâté using the classic French technique I learned at Café Boulud, but sub in Southern flavors with chicken livers and rustic jam from my backyard fig tree. I spread this pâté like butter on crunchy bread, top it with fig jam, and sprinkle it with Maldon salt for the perfect haute-humble snack.

FOR THE PÂTÉ

8 Tbsp [115 g] unsalted butter, at room temperature

2 lb [900 g] chicken livers, rinsed thoroughly, then drained

1 cup [150 g] chopped onion

2 tsp minced garlic

1 shot cognac

¾ cup [180 ml] chicken stock or broth

1 sprig fresh thyme

FOR THE FIG JAM

3 lb [1.2 kg] fresh figs, washed, stems removed

2 cups [200 g] sugar

Zest and juice of 1 lemon

FOR SERVING

White, rustic whole wheat, or sourdough all work well

5 blackberries, halved (optional)

5 figs, halved (optional)

Arugula (optional)

Shaved radish (optional)

Finishing-quality olive oil

To make the pâté: In a medium sauté pan over medium heat, melt 4 Tbsp of the butter, then add the chicken livers. Sauté the livers until just cooked, flipping halfway. Remove the livers and set aside.

Add the onion and garlic and cook over low heat for 3 to 5 minutes, or until tender and translucent. Deglaze the pan with the cognac.

Return the livers to the pan. Add the stock and thyme and let simmer for 12 to 15 minutes.

Drain and remove the thyme sprig. Transfer the solids to a food processor and add the remaining butter while processing. Purée until completely smooth.

Spread the pâté 1 in [2.5 cm] thick in a casserole dish or loaf pan and place plastic wrap on top so it is touching the pâté surface. This prevents oxidation. Let chill completely (1 to 2 hours) before serving. Serve immediately or refrigerate in an airtight container for up to 3 days.

To make the jam: Place a plate in the refrigerator. In a large saucepan over medium-low heat, combine the figs, sugar, and lemon zest and juice. Bring to a simmer, stirring constantly.

Lower the heat to low and continue to simmer, halfway off the heat, for 45 minutes to 1 hour. Stir frequently, making sure the bottom does not burn. The jam should be thick but not stiff. To test the consistency, when you think the jam is done, remove the chilled plate from the refrigerator, use a spoon to spread a thin line of jam on the plate, then run your finger through the jam. When it holds a firm edge and has a slightly wrinkled texture, it is done. Refrigerate in an airtight container for up to 2 weeks, or to store at room temperature for up to 6 months, follow the Canning 101 procedure (page 34).

To serve: I like my pâté best on toast. Remove the crust from your bread of choice and cut the bread into uniform triangles. Lightly toast the bread, then spread a layer of pâté and jam on each triangle. Garnish with halved blackberries or figs, arugula, and/or shaved radish, then drizzle olive oil over the top.

Bomb Nachos

8 TO 10 SERVINGS

My girls' group inspired this entire chapter. We started out as a few young women who would meet once a month, alternating houses and sharing potluck dishes. Dinners were late, drinks were ample, and conversation was adults-only. Our group is now a strong, close-knit crew of twelve women who have carried, showered, birthed, prayed over, cried for, and nurtured sixteen babies together. We've survived infertility, miscarriages, and devastating loss. We've guided, supported, and celebrated each other's careers. We've been secret-keepers, protectors, and healers. By sharing both the mundane and the profound, we've created a steadfast bond and unwavering support system. I doubt I'll ever be able to adequately show my gratitude for each of these women, but I'll continue to try my damnedest, one plate of their favorite, flavorful nachos at a time.

FOR THE SPANISH BOLOGNESE

2 lb [900 g] ground beef, pork, or turkey

½ cup [120 ml] olive oil

1 cup [150 g] chopped onion

½ cup [75 g] chopped bell pepper (any variety)

2 garlic cloves, minced

2 Tbsp tomato paste

½ cup [120 ml] red wine vinegar

4 cups [960 ml] classic salsa, store-bought

1 tsp cumin

1 tsp smoked paprika

1 tsp garlic powder

1 tsp onion powder

Salt

FOR THE FAJITA VEGGIES

3 cups [450 g] thinly sliced bell peppers (any variety)

3 cups [450 g] thinly sliced onions

1 cup [240 ml] olive oil

1 tsp smoked paprika

1 tsp garlic powder

Salt

FOR THE NACHOS

Two 16 oz [450 g] bags tortilla chips, from your local Mexican restaurant or grocery store

2 cups [440 g] canned black beans, drained and rinsed

Salt

4 cups [960 g] queso fresco

2 cups [475 ml] queso cheese dip, store-bought, melted

3 cups [720 ml] Homemade Salsa (recipe follows) or store-bought salsa

1 cup [240 g] sour cream

1 cup [150 g] sliced fresh jalapeño peppers

4 cups [150 g] shredded iceberg lettuce

1 cup [20 g] cilantro leaves, packed

1 cup [150 g] diced or thinly sliced English cucumbers

1 cup [150 g] diced or thinly sliced radishes

2 whole avocados, thinly sliced

1 bunch green onions, thinly sliced

3 limes, cut into wedges

cont'd

To make the bolognese: In a large sauté pan over medium-high heat, brown the meat, stirring frequently with a wooden spoon, for 10 to 12 minutes, or until just cooked through. Remove the meat and set aside.

In the same pan, combine the oil, onion, peppers, and garlic and sauté over low heat for 8 to 10 minutes, or until the onions are translucent.

With the heat still on low, add the tomato paste and stir to coat the onions and peppers. Turn up the heat to high and deglaze the pan with the red wine vinegar, scraping the bottom of the pan to remove browned bits. Cook for 2 more minutes, or until the vinegar has almost evaporated.

Add the salsa, 2 cups [480 ml] of water, the meat, cumin, paprika, and garlic and onion powders and let simmer over medium heat for 20 to 30 minutes, or until the sauce has thickened and reduced, leaving very little liquid in the pan. Season with salt.

To make the veggies: In a large sauté pan over high heat, sauté the peppers and onions with olive oil, stirring frequently to avoid sticking, for 12 to 15 minutes, or until the onions are golden brown. Remove from the heat and stir in the paprika and garlic powder. Season with salt.

To assemble the nachos: Preheat the oven to 350°F [175°C].

On two half-sheet pans, spread out the chips. Evenly layer the Spanish Bolognese, Fajita Veggies, and black beans over the chips, then add a few more chips to create more crunch, and sprinkle with salt. Sprinkle with the crumbled queso fresco and drizzle 1 cup [240 g] of the warmed queso cheese dip over the top. Bake for 5 to 8 minutes, or until the cheese is just melted.

After removing the chips from the oven, spoon the salsa over the top, then add dollops of sour cream, and drizzle with the remaining warm queso cheese dip. Layer with jalapeños, then iceberg lettuce. Evenly sprinkle with the cilantro, cucumber, and radish. Add slices of avocado and top with green onions. Serve on trays with lime wedges on the side. I typically offer forks and knives for eating, as these nachos are the quintessential beautiful mess.

VARIATION   Smoked Nachos

Sub your favorite smoked meat from your local barbecue shop for the Spanish Bolognese, drizzle the nachos with ½ cup [120 ml] of your favorite barbecue sauce, and you've got the best Tex-Mex mashup of all time.

Homemade Salsa

—— MAKES 4 CUPS [960 ML] SALSA

One 28 oz [790 g] can crushed tomatoes

One 7 oz [200 g] can chipotle
peppers in adobo sauce

½ cup [75 g] chopped red onion

¼ cup [35 g] chopped jalapeño pepper

¼ cup [5 g] cilantro leaves, packed

¼ cup [60 ml] red wine vinegar

2 garlic cloves

1 Tbsp salt

1 tsp smoked paprika

Combine all the ingredients in a food processor and process to the desired consistency. I prefer mine smooth with some texture. To stock your pantry, can the salsa in batches following the instructions in Canning 101 (page 34).

67

Sparkling Jalapeño Margarita

4 SERVINGS

This easy sipper is the most popular cocktail at KBC, where, much to my chagrin, it is known as "The Kelsey Margarita." I started making these every Thursday at our *Top Chef* viewing parties. Each week the restaurant would fill up with excited fans, camera crews, news anchors, and even the mayor, all of whom could watch each episode and simultaneously scrutinize my every reaction as I watched alongside. It was quite the party for them; for me, not so much. I spent the duration of these parties a ball of anxious nerves, just praying they didn't show the time I fell on my ass, got into a spat with another competitor, cried *again*, fell on my ass *again*, spoke out of line, and at least one hundred other less-than-flattering moments that I am obviously not going to make public now. Enter: my Sparkling Jalapeño Margarita. Tequila was needed, sparkling water made the next day a little less painful, and the lack of sugar prevented a hangover.

3 Tbsp minced jalapeño pepper, from about 1 pepper

1 tsp salt

¼ tsp freshly grated horseradish

4 oz [120 ml] agave syrup

8 oz [240 ml] mezcal tequila

4 oz [120 ml] fresh lime juice

32 oz [940 ml] Topo Chico sparkling mineral water

4 Tbsp [50 g] Tajín Clásico seasoning

In a small pitcher, muddle the jalapeño, a pinch of the salt, the horseradish, and agave syrup with a muddler or wooden spoon. Stir in the tequila, lime juice, and mineral water and set aside.

Pour a little water onto a flat plate with a rim. On another plate wider than your glass, mix the Tajín Clásico seasoning with the remaining salt. To coat the rims of the glasses, dip each in water and then in the Tajín mixture. Fill the glasses with ice and pour in the drink mixture. Enjoy immediately.

> **★ NOTE ★**
>
> If you aren't a fan of mezcal, replace with a nice reposado. The best margarita starts with good tequila, so don't reach for the bottom shelf on this one.

Meyer Lemonade

4 SERVINGS

In the South, celebratory showers are a way of life. We shower third babies, high school graduations, pageant sendoffs, and, of course, marriages—any reason to throw a party! When Deavours and I got engaged, we requested a garden engagement shower. We had just purchased our house and were eager to start landscaping. We sketched a landscape design, registered for the blooms we desired most, and could not wait to plant our dream. Our family and friends amazed us. We walked into a greenhouse of a party. There were white hydrangeas, boxwoods and small magnolia trees, gardenias, star jasmine, and azalea dogwoods. To our surprise, there was also a collection of Meyer lemon, lime, and orange trees. This unplanned patch of citrus became even more special when we learned that our grandmothers had been the dream weavers of this delightful gift.

Seven years later, we have eight trees that produce far more than we can consume and that I can glimpse out of my kitchen window every morning. In the winter, the neighborhood kids frequently come over to pick the fruit. We moms will make lemonade for the kids and a pitcher of cocktails for ourselves. It tickles me to think that this is exactly what our grandmothers dreamed for us all along.

½ cup [100 g] sugar

1 cup [240 ml] fresh Meyer lemon juice

In a small pot over medium heat, stir together the sugar and 1 cup [240 ml] of water until the sugar dissolves. Let cool, then add the juice and an additional 4 cups [960 ml] of water. Fill four glasses with crushed ice and divide the lemonade among the glasses.

VARIATION   Meyer Lemonade Cocktail

To make it a cocktail, in a medium pitcher, combine the Meyer Lemonade, 4 oz [120 ml] of grapefruit vodka, and 5 drops of orange blossom water and stir. Divide among four glasses filled with crushed ice, garnished with cucumber and mint.

VARIATION   Meyer Lemonade Shandy

Or turn this into the best homemade shandy by stirring in a 12 oz [355 ml] bottle of your favorite light beer and serving as directed above. The bubbles mixed with fresh lemon are like fireworks in your mouth and make the most refreshing drink on a hot summer day.

➤ NOTE ◄

Don't let your backyard citrus be just a winter thing. Juice your fruits, freeze the juice in ice cube trays, then store the cubes in airtight bags in your freezer to use all year round.

Grown-Up Shirley Temple

1 SERVING

When I was growing up, our family rarely ate out. Sunday was the exception. Every week after church, we were lucky enough to head to the country club for brunch, where we always sat at the same table. Stella, our very favorite server, would make us Shirley Temples with extra cherries and place them at our seats before we arrived. As a child, this thoughtful gesture made me feel so special and known. I remind myself often of her hospitality, and I try to emulate it for my guests.

These grown-up versions are really fun to make for a small party. Line up all your best flutes, add the fixins, and pour champagne as guests are arriving.

2 bourbon cherries, plus 2 oz [60 ml] syrup, preferably Jack Rudy Bourbon Cocktail Cherries

2 or 3 drops orange bitters

5 oz [150 ml] champagne

1 lime wedge

Drop the cherries and bitters in the bottom of a champagne flute, then add the syrup. Fill with the champagne and squeeze the lime wedge into the flute.

71

Savannah Peach Sangria

4 TO 6 SERVINGS

When Deavours and I were dating, we visited Savannah for a long weekend. Back then, we'd frequently run off for a weekend of fun in a place we hadn't been together. We stopped in the central market of town to sit on a bench, listen to live music, and sip homemade Georgia peach sangria. Deavours snapped a picture of me that still makes me smile. I had on a straw hat, big sunglasses, a baby face, and windblown hair. My head is back, laughing—at what, I can't recall. I love remembering those blissful days of dating, and the flavors in this drink bring them all back.

3 cups [570 g] sliced ripe peaches

4 oz [120 ml] Aperol

2 Tbsp agave syrup, plus more to taste

4 oz [120 ml] peach schnapps

4 oz [120 ml] Pinot Grigio or Sauvignon Blanc

2 cups [380 g] frozen cherries

1 bottle [750 ml] brut champagne, cava, or prosecco

Place the peaches, Aperol, and agave syrup in a large pitcher. Muddle with a muddler or wooden spoon for about 1 minute, until mostly mashed. Add the schnapps and muddle for 30 seconds to combine. Add the wine and cherries. Taste and add additional agave syrup if you like it sweeter.

When ready to serve, fill Collins glasses with ice, then fill each glass halfway with the mixture. Top with champagne and gently stir. The sangria will keep refrigerated in an airtight container for up to 2 days.

KBC Spicy Bloody Mary

4 TO 6 SERVINGS

It's no secret that the hair of the dog does the trick the day after a wild night. KBC's Spicy Bloody Mary kicks it up a notch and delivers the magic cure. Every Saturday, guests line up to enjoy our biscuits and Bloody Marys. Though we've moved, remodeled, revamped, and expanded, we've never altered this recipe, and it's rarely met a critic.

One 32 oz [960 ml] bottle tomato juice

8 oz [240 ml] high-quality vodka

1 Tbsp Worcestershire sauce

1 tsp freshly grated horseradish

½ tsp celery salt

½ tsp freshly ground black pepper

⅛ tsp soy sauce

4 to 6 dashes Tabasco hot sauce

1 lime, cut into 4 to 6 wedges

Tajín Clásico seasoning, for the rim

4 to 6 slices pickled jalapeño rings

4 to 6 pimiento olives

4 to 6 pickled okra

4 to 6 pickled green beans

4 to 12 celery stalks

In a medium pitcher, stir together the tomato juice, vodka, Worcestershire, horseradish, celery salt, pepper, soy sauce, and Tabasco until combined.

For each serving, squeeze a lime wedge into an empty Ball jar or Collins glass, then run the wedge around the rim. Spread a layer of Tajín seasoning on a plate and dip the rim to completely coat. Drop a lime wedge into the glass, fill with ice, and then pour in the Bloody Mary mixture to the top.

Skewer 1 jalapeño ring, 1 olive, 1 okra, and 1 green bean on a bamboo stick and place in the glass with a celery stalk or two. Repeat with the remaining glasses.

Bourbon Cider Mimosas

6 TO 8 SERVINGS

Owning a restaurant means dreaming big and having a lot of faith. For five years, I dreamed of opening a full bar at KBC where gregarious bartenders behind a long marble bar would shake specialty cocktails. When that dream finally became a reality in December 2019, this is the first recipe I crafted for those smiling bartenders to serve!

2 qt [1.9 L] apple cider

Juice and strips of peel from 2 oranges

4 sticks Mexican cinnamon

½ cup [50 g] star anise

6 to 8 whole cloves

16 oz [480 ml] bourbon

1 bottle [750 ml] champagne

1 cup [150 g] fresh cranberries, halved

In a medium saucepan over medium-high heat, combine the cider, orange juice, cinnamon, star anise, and cloves. Bring to a boil, then lower the heat and let simmer for 20 minutes. Remove from the heat and stir in the bourbon. Chill in the refrigerator until cool, 20 to 30 minutes.

For each serving, pour 2 oz [60 ml] of the spiked cider into a flute or coupe glass, then top with champagne. Garnish with an orange peel, star anise, and cranberry halves.

Pirates Cove Bushwacker

6 TO 8 SERVINGS

When I was growing up, we were fortunate that my family had a beach house on Ono Island, a small spit of land at the mouth of Perdido Bay on the northern Gulf of Mexico. Both my parents grew up in Mobile, Alabama. My mom had spent her childhood weekends at her grandparents' house on Dog River, about an hour away from our beach house. My mom's family shared a lot of stories growing up, but their best memories were centered around their days on Dog River. Fishing all day, setting crab traps for supper, swimming at night, and chasing cousins around the sand dunes. Years later, my cousins and I played in the same sand on the same water, carrying out the same traditions as our parents.

There was one restaurant nearby, Pirates Cove, an old marina-turned-pit-stop famous for their burgers and bushwackers—milkshakes with a little something added for the grown-ups. We'd pull our boat up and swim to the dock, where we'd eat burgers in our swimsuits while our parents sipped on milkshakes we weren't allowed to have. Years later, I finally figured out why they giggled so much after those little lunch trips.

2 scoops vanilla ice cream

One 15 oz [450 ml] can cream of coconut

4 oz [120 ml] bourbon

4 oz [120 ml] dark rum

3 oz [90 ml] Kahlúa

1 banana, frozen

1 Tbsp chocolate syrup, plus more for garnish

Maraschino cherries, for garnish

Fill a blender halfway with ice, then add the ice cream, cream of coconut, bourbon, rum, Kahlúa, banana, and chocolate syrup. Blend until smooth. To serve, drizzle syrup around the side of a glass, pour in the frozen mixture to the brim, and top with 1 or 2 cherries. Enjoy immediately.

No. 2

Alabama Salad with Cucumber Skin Green Goddess Dressing

4 TO 6 SERVINGS

There is a standard salad in the South, and if you've been here, you know what I'm talkin' about. It is the start of every steakhouse, fine dining, banquet, or mother-in-law's dinner. Iceberg lettuce, bacon bits, shredded Cheddar cheese, croutons, and a single mealy cherry tomato, all heavily doused in ranch. The timeless, consistent, nutrient-deficient salad bar salad. While I've developed a taste for more robust greens, I still have a nostalgic fondness for this Southern staple. I've revamped it to add flavor, and at KBC we top it with sautéed shrimp or snapper. Judge all you want—it's pretty damn good, y'all.

1 cucumber

¼ cup [60 ml] apple cider vinegar

½ tsp sugar

¼ tsp salt, plus more to taste

4 cups [720 g] cubed French bread

1 cup [240 ml] olive oil

1 head iceberg lettuce

3 cups [450 g] cherry tomatoes, halved vertically

5 slices cooked bacon, chopped

½ cup [55 g] shaved Parmesan cheese

Cucumber Skin Green Goddess Dressing (recipe follows)

¼ cup [60 ml] balsamic vinegar

¼ cup [25 g] slivered green onion

10 to 15 turns freshly ground black pepper

Peel the cucumber, reserving the skins for the dressing, and cut it into half moons. Toss the slices with the apple cider vinegar, sugar, and salt and set aside. Drain before using.

Preheat the oven to 375°F [190°C] and line a sheet pan with parchment paper. In a mixing bowl, toss the bread with ½ cup [120 ml] of the olive oil and a sprinkle of salt. Bake on the prepared pan for 10 to 15 minutes, or until toasted and golden. Set aside.

Cut the lettuce into 4 to 6 large wedges. Assemble the salad on a large platter or individually on salad plates, with a wedge on each plate, as follows: lettuce wedge, tomatoes, cucumber slices, bacon, croutons, and Parmesan. Drizzle heavily with the Cucumber Skin Green Goddess Dressing, then the remaining olive oil and the balsamic. Garnish with the green onion and pepper.

Cucumber Skin Green Goddess Dressing
—— 2 CUPS [480 ML]

Skins from 1 cucumber

1 cup [240 g] mayonnaise

½ cup [120 g] sour cream

½ cup [75 g] roughly chopped onion

¼ cup [5 g] fresh flat-leaf parsley leaves

3 Tbsp fresh dill fronds

1 Tbsp white vinegar

1 garlic clove

1 tsp freshly ground black pepper

¼ tsp celery salt

¼ to ½ cup [60 to 120 ml] buttermilk

Salt

Combine the cucumber skins, mayonnaise, sour cream, onion, parsley, dill, white vinegar, garlic clove, pepper, and celery salt in a food processor. While processing, slowly and sparingly add the buttermilk until the dressing is completely smooth and thin enough to drizzle but not as thin as water. Taste and season with salt, if needed.

85

Birthday Pickled Salad

5 SERVINGS

As children, we were taught to eat what's in front of us. "I'm not a short order cook," our mom would say. The only exception was on our birthday—then we could pick anything we wanted. It was a special day, and she always made sure we felt it. Funny enough, each of us always chose the same down-to-earth, sensible meal: boiled artichokes with butter, a big, fat grilled steak, and Mom's pickled salad. Looking back, I see the power of a mother's influence—it's there even when you think you're the one making the decisions.

3 cups [450 g] cucumbers, cut into ¼ in [6 mm] thick half-moons

½ cup [75 g] thinly sliced onion

2 avocados, cut into ½ in [12 mm] wedges

2 cups tomatoes, cut into ½ in [12 mm] thick half-moons

½ cup [120 ml] red wine vinegar

Morton Nature's Seasons

Layer the salad, alternating cucumber, onion, avocado, and tomato, spiraling from the edges of the bowl in to the middle. Drizzle vinegar all over and sprinkle liberally with Morton Nature's Seasons. Let sit for 15 minutes before serving.

······ NOTE ······

I make an exception to my preference for fresh herbs in this recipe. The power of nostalgia is strong, and my mom always finished this dish with a big old sprinkle of this seasoned mixture. I don't use this seasoning anywhere else, but my mom never made this dish without it, and I don't either.

BLT Butter Bean Salad

4 TO 6 SERVINGS

Since the year I got engaged, I've hosted an annual Mother's Day brunch to celebrate all the matriarchs in our family. I set the table with the nice china, polish Grandma's silver, and have flower arrangements piled on the kitchen counter, waiting to be gifted. My Grandmother June and Deavours's Mimi each played big roles in our lives and passed within a month of each other. On their last Mother's Day brunch I was days away from giving birth to my first child, and we were in the middle of a move, surviving off a few mixing bowls, a skillet, and a coffee machine. I could barely muster up the energy to cook a meal and just about pulled the plug on this annual gathering. Thankfully, my love for keeping traditions got the best of me. I focused on keeping it simple with crowd-pleasers I could whip up with my eyes closed: BLT Butter Bean Salad, Bee's Fried Chicken (page 181), and Banana Cream Pie (page 234).

Over these basics, my favorite mothers and grandmothers shared stories of their pregnancies, childbirths, and babies—smiling at the good and chuckling together at the bad. It was one of those days where things couldn't have gone better. I've kept the menu the same ever since, and each year I am flooded with the fondest memories of that golden day.

3 cups [435 g] baby butter beans, fresh or frozen

10 slices thick-sliced, applewood smoked bacon

3 cups [720 ml] chicken stock or broth

1 head Bibb or butter lettuce

3 heirloom tomatoes, cut into medium wedges

¼ cup [25 g] crumbled gorgonzola cheese

½ cup [120 ml] finishing-quality olive oil

¼ cup [60 ml] apple cider vinegar

¼ cup [5 g] chiffonade fresh basil

¼ cup [5 g] chopped fresh flat-leaf parsley

Salt and freshly ground black pepper

In a medium sauce pot over medium heat, combine the beans, 1 slice of the bacon, and the chicken stock. Bring to a slow simmer and cook for 15 to 20 minutes, or until tender. Blanch by straining the beans and submerging them in ice-cold water for 10 minutes, or until cool throughout, then drain and spread on paper towels to absorb excess liquid. Set aside.

Cook the remaining bacon slices in a skillet over medium-low heat for 15 to 20 minutes, flipping halfway, or until crisp on both sides. Remove the bacon, then roughly chop to a medium dice. Reserve the bacon fat.

Layer whole lettuce leaves across the bottom of a wide salad bowl or a medium platter with a lip. Top with the beans, tomatoes, cheese, and then bacon. Drizzle with the reserved bacon fat, olive oil, and apple cider vinegar. Top with the basil, parsley, and salt and pepper. Let sit for 10 to 15 minutes before serving, but no more. If making ahead, place the undressed salad in the refrigerator. Drizzle with the bacon fat, oil, and vinegar just before serving.

Cornbread Panzanella Salad

4 TO 6 SERVINGS

In Italy, this salad was created to use up stale baguettes left over from the day before. In the South, we are more likely to have day-old cornbread. I make cornbread as a side with collards and soups, so this is a predictable day-after treat.

3 cups [450 g] stale Fried Cornbread (page 108), cut into a medium dice

½ cup [120 ml] finishing-quality olive oil

¼ cup [60 ml] balsamic vinegar

1 tsp salt

½ cup [75 g] diced bell pepper, yellow or green

1 large tomato, chopped

¼ cup [35 g] thinly sliced red onion

10 basil leaves, chiffonade

Freshly ground black pepper

▄ NOTE ▄

This is one of my favorite summer dishes to throw together. I usually have an abundance of peppers from the garden and tomatoes sitting on the counter. I love pairing it with grilled steak or fish and calling it a day.

To begin, be sure your cornbread is good and stale. It should be hard all the way through. If it's not, spread the cornbread out on a sheet pan and bake at 325°F [165°C] for 15 minutes, or until crunchy like a crouton. Let cool.

In a medium or large mixing bowl, whisk together the olive oil, vinegar, and salt. Add the cornbread and toss to fully coat, then add the bell pepper, tomato, and onion and toss again. Top with the basil leaves and black pepper and adjust the seasoning. Serve immediately—this salad becomes soggy if it sits too long.

Slaw

Slaw is what you assign the least talented or downright bad cook to bring to the potluck. It requires little to no skill, and these days it even comes in little premade kits that are foolproof. That said, I respect a great coleslaw, and I expect any decent Southern cook to have a recipe in their back pocket. I like mine two ways—vinegar based, with a little sweet tang, and Southern style, heavy on the celery seed. When done well, slaw can provide an excellent accompaniment to many mains. It adds texture, fat, and acidity to the plate—three of the five qualities that make a well-balanced dish. Let these two versions serve as your back-pocket recipes.

—✦ NOTE ✦—

We use slaw *a lot* at KBC. Here are a few of my favorite ways to use slaw beyond the side dish:

Sauté Vinegar Slaw, toss with black-eyed peas, and serve with seared pork chops.

Top Bee's Fried Chicken (page 181) with Southern Slaw, Cucumber Skin Green Goddess Dressing (page 85), and pickles in a potato bun.

Top Vinegar Slaw with brisket, barbecue sauce, and hot sauce.

Add 1 Tbsp of sesame oil and a handful of green onions to Vinegar Slaw and toss with chopped leftover roasted chicken.

Southern Slaw
— 6 TO 8 SERVINGS

One 16 oz [455 g] bag shredded cabbage mix

¼ cup [35 g] thinly sliced bell pepper

2 Tbsp thinly sliced red onion

1 cup [240 g] mayonnaise

¼ cup [60 ml] red wine vinegar

2 Tbsp vegetable oil

1 Tbsp honey

1 Tbsp celery seed

1 tsp salt

5 turns freshly ground black pepper

In a large mixing bowl, toss all the ingredients together. Refrigerate for 30 minutes to chill. The slaw can be refrigerated in a covered bowl for up to 2 days before serving.

Vinegar Slaw
— 6 TO 8 SERVINGS

One 16 oz [455 g] bag shredded cabbage mix

¼ cup [35 g] sauerkraut, store-bought

¼ cup [35 g] thinly sliced bell pepper

2 Tbsp thinly sliced red onion

¼ cup [60 ml] red wine vinegar

2 Tbsp vegetable oil

1 Tbsp honey

1 tsp salt

5 turns freshly ground black pepper

In a large mixing bowl, toss all the ingredients together. Refrigerate for 30 minutes to chill. The slaw can be refrigerated in a covered bowl for up to 2 days before serving.

Squash, Onions, and Brown Butter

3 TO 5 SERVINGS

There are quite a few Southern vegetable recipes that would absolutely mortify the classically trained French chefs who taught me. These recipes disregard proper cooking techniques, but they are freaking delicious. In this one, we cook these babies down so much they are hardly recognizable as squash. The rebel in me finds this recipe particularly satisfying.

5 Tbsp [70 g] unsalted butter

4 cups [600 g] thinly sliced onion

6 medium yellow summer squash, cut into ½ in [12 mm] half-moons (equal to roughly 10 cups [1 kg])

1 tsp onion powder

1 tsp garlic powder

10 to 15 turns freshly ground black pepper

1½ to 2 tsp salt

In a Dutch oven or large cast iron skillet, melt the butter and add the onions, squash, and seasonings. Let cook down over medium heat for about 10 minutes. The squash will release their liquid and the mixture will shrink to almost half its size. Lower the heat to low and stir every few minutes. You're trying to create caramelization slowly, so don't freak if the veggies stick to the pan a bit. Let cook for 45 minutes, stirring frequently and scraping the bottom often. This dish is done when it's cooked down by at least two-thirds in volume and is golden. Transfer to a serving dish and serve warm.

Street Corn

When you work in a Michelin-star restaurant, you learn just as much upstairs with world-renowned chefs as you do downstairs in the prep quarters. Upstairs, they taught me about finesse and skill; downstairs, I learned about flavor, speed, and efficiency. At Café Boulud, besides peeling buckets of garlic, dicing gallons of potatoes, and slicing perfect disks of butternut squash, I was also tasked with doing whatever Grande told me to do. Grande was the resident butcher and, to be honest, the freaking boss. I was the only woman in the kitchen, young and naïve, and Grande quickly took me under his wing and spent a lot of time showing me how to make his best dishes, which the staff ate family-style before the restaurant opened each night. His cilantro-lime corn was my favorite.

I make two versions: If we are eating from the grill, I grill the cobs too; if we're cooking in the kitchen, I use a skillet and cook just the kernels. Both are delicious!

Grilled Street Corn
—— 4 SERVINGS

4 sweet corn cobs, shucked, cut in half

½ cup [115 g] unsalted butter, at room temperature

8 tsp Tajín Clásico seasoning

1 lime

Salt

½ cup [10 g] chopped cilantro

½ cup [25 g] chiffonade green onion

½ cup [50 g] queso fresco

Heat the grill to 350°F to 375°F [175°C to 190°C]. Tear off eight sheets of foil large enough to wrap around a half cob. Lay a cob on each piece of foil in an assembly line. Spread 1 Tbsp of butter on each cob, sprinkle 1 tsp of Tajín seasoning over each, squeeze the lime evenly over the cobs, and sprinkle with salt. Wrap the corn tightly in the foil, like a burrito, and make sure the ends are sealed. Grill, rotating frequently, for 10 to 15 minutes, or until the corn begins to pop. Let sit in the foil off the heat for 15 minutes. Open the foil, then top with the cilantro, green onion, and queso fresco. Serve warm.

Skillet Street Corn
—— 4 TO 6 SERVINGS

2 Tbsp unsalted butter

4 cups [600 g] fresh sweet corn kernels

Salt

½ cup [50 g] chiffonade green onion

Zest and juice of 1 lime

1 Tbsp Tajín Clásico seasoning

¼ tsp smoked paprika

1 Tbsp mayonnaise

½ cup [10 g] chopped cilantro

½ cup [50 g] queso fresco

In a medium or large skillet over medium-high heat, melt the butter, then add the corn kernels and sprinkle with salt. Cook, stirring frequently, for 10 to 15 minutes, or until the corn has browned slightly and begins to pop. Lower the heat to medium-low and add the green onion, lime juice, Tajín seasoning, and smoked paprika. Let cool for 15 minutes and then fold in the mayonnaise. Taste and season with more salt if needed. Top with the cilantro, queso fresco, and lime zest. Serve warm.

Tomato Pie

6 TO 8 SERVINGS

In a community where a plate of food isn't a meal if it's not the ole meat-n-three, the tomato pie goes against the odds. She's the one who broke the glass ceiling and managed to get rugged farmers with callused hands to cheerfully sit down to a vegetarian meal of pie.

My spin on this classic pie includes roasting sour green tomatoes and leaving the cherry tomatoes raw, adding caramelized onions for good measure, and piling on the cheese. If you don't have time or just don't feel like making your own crust, then don't. Pillsbury has that thing down pat these days, and I'll go on record saying that, to be honest, it's pretty damn good.

FOR THE RAW TOMATOES

3 cups [450 g] halved cherry tomatoes

½ tsp sugar

Salt

FOR THE ROASTED GREEN TOMATOES

4 cups [600 g] 1 in [2.5 cm] green tomatoes, cut into cubes

3 Tbsp olive oil

½ tsp sugar

Salt

FOR THE CARAMELIZED ONIONS

2 Tbsp unsalted butter

1 cup [150 g] thinly sliced onion

FOR ASSEMBLY

⅓ cup [7 g] fresh basil leaves

1 tsp fresh thyme leaves

8 to 10 turns freshly ground black pepper

Salt

½ cup [120 g] mayonnaise

⅓ cup [35 g] freshly grated smoked Gouda

⅓ cup [35 g] freshly grated Parmesan

One 10 in [25 cm] piecrust, Classic Pie Dough (page 231) or store-bought, blind-baked

Preheat the oven to 400°F [205°C].

To make the raw tomatoes: In a medium mixing bowl, toss the cherry tomatoes with the sugar and a sprinkle of salt. Place them in a colander to drain.

To make the roasted green tomatoes: In a large mixing bowl, toss the green tomatoes with the olive oil, sugar, and a sprinkle of salt. Line a sheet pan with parchment paper. Spread the tomatoes on the parchment in a single layer and bake on the middle rack of the oven for 20 to 30 minutes, or until they are dried out and slightly browned. Drain the excess liquid from the pan.

To caramelize the onions: In a large saucepan over medium-low heat, melt the butter, then add the onions and cook, stirring frequently, for 8 to 10 minutes, or until they are a medium brown. If they burn or get too dark, add a splash of water, scrape up the dark bits, and continue cooking to reduce the liquid.

To assemble: Preheat the oven to 350°F [175°C]. In a large mixing bowl, gently stir together the onions, drained raw tomatoes, roasted tomatoes, basil, thyme, black pepper, and a sprinkle of salt. In a separate medium mixing bowl, stir together the mayonnaise, Gouda, and Parmesan. Spoon the tomato mixture into the blind-baked piecrust, then top with the mayo and cheese filling. Bake on the middle rack of the oven for 25 to 30 minutes, or until the cheese is golden and the pie is slightly firm in middle. Let sit at room temperature for 30 minutes before cutting.

This is a great recipe for using up those not-so-great, overripe cherry tomatoes. I enjoy this dish most when topped with an arugula or frisée salad. Simply toss together ½ cup [10 g] of lettuce with a squeeze of fresh lemon juice, a dash of salt, and a drizzle of finishing-quality olive oil to make each slice a full meal.

Squash Casserole

4 TO 6 SERVINGS

Every Southerner I know has a special family squash casserole recipe, but to achieve the perfect squash casserole, it must pass these three tests:

Crust: The crust must be golden, crispy, and cheesy. Cheese and crust must be in perfect harmony; cheese shall not overwhelm crust.

Squash cookery: Squash must be caramelized and cooked prior to joining forces with other casserole ingredients. Please do not think you can skip the two-cook method. It matters.

Casserole consistency: The casserole must be set, but not firm, and there should not be any liquid at the bottom of the dish. The dish should be comparable in texture to a perfectly made custard or egg casserole.

8 Tbsp [115 g] unsalted butter, plus more for greasing the dish

4 cups [600 g] thinly sliced onion

6 medium yellow squash, sliced into ½ in [12 mm] half-moons

3 tsp salt

2 large eggs, beaten

1¼ cups [300 g] mayonnaise

1 cup [240 g] sour cream

1 cup [100 g] freshly grated extra sharp Cheddar cheese

5 to 8 turns freshly ground black pepper

¼ cup [30 g] fine ground cornmeal, for dusting the dish

1 cup [100 g] panko bread crumbs

½ cup [50 g] freshly grated Parmesan

½ cup [50 g] freshly grated Gruyère

Preheat the oven to 350°F [175°C]. Melt 4 Tbsp [58 g] of the butter in a large skillet or Dutch oven over medium heat and add the onions, squash, and half of the salt. Cook for about 10 minutes. The squash will release its liquid and the mixture will cook down by about half. Lower the heat to low and cook for 30 minutes, stirring frequently and scraping the bottom often. You'll know it's done when the veggies are golden.

In a medium-large mixing bowl, mix together the eggs, mayonnaise, sour cream, Cheddar, pepper, and the remaining salt. Gently fold in the squash mixture, being careful not to mash the squash. Taste the mixture and adjust the seasonings.

Butter a 2 qt [1.9 L] casserole dish and dust with the cornmeal. Pour in the squash mixture. Melt the remaining 4 Tbsp [58 g] of butter. In a medium mixing bowl, toss together the panko, Parmesan, Gruyère, and melted butter. Top the casserole with the panko mixture. Bake for 20 to 30 minutes, or until golden brown on top, bubbling, and brown on the edges.

VARIATION   Corn Casserole

This recipe doubles as a base for some of my other favorite veggie casseroles.

Sub 8 cups [1.2 kg] of fresh corn kernels for the squash. Sweat the onions in butter over medium heat for 20 minutes, then add the corn, turn the heat to high, and blister for 5 minutes. Follow the remaining steps as directed.

VARIATION   Green Bean Casserole

Sub 10 cups [1.5 kg] of fresh green beans for the squash. Blanch the green beans in a medium-large pot and set aside. Melt the butter in large skillet, add the onions and green beans, and cook over medium heat for 20 minutes, or until the beans have withered slightly and the onions have lightly caramelized. Follow the remaining steps as directed.

Twinkle Light Succotash

4 TO 6 SERVINGS

I always pictured my future as a house. A crowded table on the porch with lights dripping from big magnolia trees was part of the vision. So before we even changed the locks on our new house, during naptime I was up on a ladder, hanging twinkle lights above the patio. We had a two-week-old baby, and Deavours thought I was crazy—I can't say I disagreed. But on that first official night in the new house, under those twinkling lights, we ate grilled steak and corn on plates and silverware rummaged from boxes and sipped champagne out of coffee cups. James Taylor cooed in the background, and Monroe slept in my arms. I looked around the big table at the seats I knew would soon be filled and soaked it in. I was home.

Now, I can't recall if I made succotash the next day (moving will throw you off like that), but usually when we have corn on the cob, I make extra so I can serve succotash with the leftovers. This version is packed with flavor and simple, but don't skip any steps. Each one is calculated to bring out the best in each ingredient.

➤ NOTE ◄

If you don't have lima beans, leave them out and you've still got a winning dish known as Corn Maque Choux.

2 cups [290 g] baby lima beans, fresh or frozen

Salt

3 Tbsp unsalted butter

½ cup [65 g] chopped Conecuh sausage

1 cup [150 g] chopped onion

¼ cup [35 g] chopped celery

¼ cup [35 g] chopped bell pepper, red or green

2 garlic cloves, minced

3 cups [435 g] fresh sweet corn kernels

1 cup [150 g] pickled okra, cut into ½ in [12 mm] rounds

1 cup [150 g] halved cherry tomatoes

1 heirloom tomato, sliced into ¼ in [6 mm] rounds (optional)

½ tsp Old Bay seasoning

¼ cup [5 g] minced flat-leaf parsley

¼ cup [25 g] chiffonade green onion

Place the lima beans in a medium saucepan and add enough water to cover by 1 in [2.5 cm]. Bring to a boil, then add a dash of salt. Lower the heat and simmer for 10 minutes. Drain and set the beans aside.

While the beans are cooking, melt the butter in a cast iron skillet over medium heat. Add the sausage and render the fat, stirring frequently, for 8 to 10 minutes. Remove the sausage and leave the fat in the skillet.

Add the onion, celery, bell pepper, and garlic and cook over low heat for 5 to 6 minutes, or until just tender. Stir in the lima beans, corn, and okra and cook for 5 to 6 minutes, or until the corn is tender and bright yellow.

Turn the heat to high, add the cherry tomatoes and tomato slices, if using, and stir constantly for 2 minutes. Season with the Old Bay and adjust the salt. Garnish with the parsley and green onion and serve.

103

Okra Hot Fries

3 TO 4 SERVINGS

We grew our first batch of okra last summer. It was rewarding to do the work ourselves and see our beautiful pods sprout. Okra grows fast, and sometimes we returned from a quick trip to the beach to find the stalks too starchy and large for most recipes. So I tried roasting them, and they were an instant hit. The first time I made these, they were supposed to be the side dish for pork tenderloin and salad. But when they came out of the oven, Deavours, Monroe, and I devoured them before they ever touched a plate. Monroe exclaimed, "Hot fries!" while he ate them—they were that good.

20 to 25 medium to large okra pods, sliced lengthwise

3 Tbsp olive oil

1 tsp garlic powder

1 tsp onion powder

1 tsp salt

¼ tsp celery seed

1 tsp Tajín Clásico seasoning (optional)

Preheat the oven to 400°F [205°C]. In a medium mixing bowl, toss the okra with the oil, garlic powder, onion powder, salt, celery seed, and Tajín, if using. On a sheet pan (or two) lined with parchment paper, space the okra out in a single layer without touching. Cook for 20 minutes, stirring halfway through. They should be brown and crispy. Serve warm as a snack or side dish with any of the following cheat sauces.

Cheat Sauces
—— **4 TO 6 SERVINGS EACH**

A cheat sauce is a chef term for a sauce made from mixing something into mayonnaise. These are your best friend in a pinch, and no one will know that you pulled it off in 17.8 seconds. I like these sauces with just about anything fried, but they really hit their high when dipped with these Okra Hot Fries or Fried Pickled Okra (page 57).

HERB CHEAT SAUCE

¾ cup [180 g] mayonnaise

¼ cup [60 g] sour cream

1 Tbsp pesto

Pinch of salt

SRIRACHA CHEAT SAUCE

1 cup [240 g] mayonnaise

3 Tbsp sriracha

1 Tbsp barbecue sauce

GARLIC CHEAT SAUCE

1 cup [240 g] mayonnaise

1 tsp granulated garlic

¼ tsp garlic powder

Pinch of salt

HOT HONEY CHEAT SAUCE

1 cup [240 g] mayonnaise

1 tsp honey

¼ tsp cayenne pepper

Pinch of smoked paprika

Pinch of salt

To make each sauce, simply whisk the ingredients together in a mixing bowl until combined. Serve immediately or store in an airtight container in the refrigerator for up to 6 days.

Black-Eyed Peas with Greens and Potlikker and Fried Cornbread

I am a product of the South, and I love my home and its food. I also abhor this region's shameful, inhumane historic practices of slavery, Jim Crow, and the de facto segregation and racism that persist today. This recipe is an incredible dish born of necessity during the darkest days of slavery. Enslaved cooks were understandably always looking for ways to put food on the table for their families. They also worked the land and therefore knew the facts of food and farming better than those who had purchased them. Enslaved cooks drained off the greens before serving their enslavers, as they knew the leftover broth could both nourish and hydrate; it was a liquid gold we now call *potlikker*. This became a staple meal served with black-eyed peas grown in a little garden and cornbread made with left-over corn mash.[1] I acknowledge the horror and sorrow slavery inflicted on millions of people and the destruction it left behind that we still grapple with today, and I have deep respect for the keen, resilient, and creative individuals who endured it and the legacies they left behind. I make this dish in their honor.

[1] *To learn more about the history of Southern food, I highly recommend the works of Edna Lewis, a champion of Southern food and its history, as well as Dora Charles's cookbook* A Real Southern Cook: In Her Savannah Kitchen *(Houghton Mifflin Harcourt, 2015).*

Black-Eyed Peas
— 4 TO 6 SERVINGS

2 Tbsp unsalted butter

1 smoked ham hock

½ cup [75 g] thinly sliced onion

6 cups [1.4 L] chicken stock or broth

2 cups [300 g] black-eyed peas, frozen and thawed or fresh

Tiny pinch of red pepper flakes

5 to 8 turns freshly ground black pepper

1 tsp salt

2 bay leaves

In a medium Dutch oven over medium-high heat, melt the butter, then add the ham hock. Sear the hock lightly, 1 to 2 minutes per side (chefs refer to this quick sear method as "kiss"). Remove the hock and sauté the onions in the fat over medium heat until slightly translucent, 10 minutes. Add the stock, peas, red pepper, black pepper, salt, and bay leaves. Bring to a boil, then lower the heat to a simmer. Cover and cook for 30 to 45 minutes, or until the peas are just tender. Cooking them too long or over high heat will cause the peas to burst. Taste and adjust the salt and serve over Greens and Potlikker (facing page) with Fried Cornbread (page 108).

Greens and Potlikker
—— 4 TO 6 SERVINGS

2 lb [900 g] collard greens

3 Tbsp unsalted butter

2 ham hocks

5 slices bacon

1 cup [150 g] thinly sliced onion

3 garlic cloves, thinly sliced

2 dried whole red peppers

¼ cup [60 ml] apple cider vinegar

4 cups [960 ml] chicken stock or broth

Pinch of red pepper flakes

1 tsp salt, plus more for seasoning

Vinegar pepper sauce, store-bought or homemade (see Note, page 108), for finishing

Prepare the collards by slicing down the sides of the stalks to remove the leafy greens. Chiffonade the leaves and dice the stalks. Keep the leaves and diced stalks separate.

In a medium Dutch oven over medium heat, melt the butter, then add the hocks and bacon, rendering the fat and slightly browning both. Remove the hocks and bacon. Add the diced collard stalks and the onions; cook in the fat over medium heat, stirring frequently, for 15 to 20 minutes, or until slightly translucent. Add the garlic and whole dried peppers and cook for 5 more minutes. Turn the heat to high and add the apple cider vinegar. Let cook for 1 minute, or until the vinegar reduces by half.

Turn the heat back down to medium, add the leafy greens, and cook for 15 minutes, or until the greens wilt slightly. Add the stock, red pepper flakes, and salt and bring to a boil. Cover, lower the heat, and let simmer for 45 minutes to 1 hour, or until the greens are dark in color and tender. Taste and adjust the salt. Top with vinegar pepper sauce to your liking and enjoy.

cont'd

Fried Cornbread
—— 3 TO 4 SERVINGS

2 cups [260 g] fine ground white cornmeal (I prefer J. T. Pollard)

Salt

Canola oil, for frying

In a medium mixing bowl, combine the cornmeal and a pinch of salt and gradually add 2 to 2½ cups [480 to 600 ml] of water, monitoring the consistency. The batter should resemble a thin pancake batter.

In a medium cast iron skillet, pour canola oil to 1½ to 2 in [3.8 to 5 cm] deep. Heat the oil over medium-high heat to about 325°F [165°C]. Line a plate with paper towels.

Spoon 1 Tbsp (heaping) of batter into the hot oil to test. The batter should spread quickly and slowly bubble, forming a flat, crispy disk. If the batter does not spread and stays round and ball-like, stir 1 Tbsp more water into the batter and test again. Fry 5 to 6 spoonfuls at a time, being sure not to overcrowd. When the disks are golden, use a slotted spoon to transfer them to the paper towels and sprinkle with salt. Eat hot.

······ NOTE ······

Down South, you don't see braised greens on the table without a jar of pepper sauce nearby. We typically make it in the summertime when we do our pickling and canning. You simply boil at least 1 cup [250 ml] of vinegar and pour it over tiny hot peppers, such as African bird's eye or Tabasco, in a jar. My grandmother always saved her tall vinegar and honey jars all year specifically to reuse them for this. I still have one of her jars in my fridge that I refresh year after year. The spicy vinegar is most commonly doused all over greens, but I use it for just about anything you can think of.

Conecuh Collards and Alabama "Spinach" Dip

If you want to get your recipe wheels turning, just overplant the bejesus out of something and voilà; necessity is the mother of invention! The first year we had our garden, I was like Oprah at Christmas: "You get some collards, you get some collards!" Friends, relatives, neighbors, the FedEx man, they all got a bag, and there were still more leaves to pick. When even the restaurant had tired of them, it was time to get creative.

I first made Conecuh Collards for my mother-in-law's birthday as a side served with whole roasted salmon and jasmine rice. She admitted that she'd never order it off a menu, yet she loved it! The next day, I added some good cheese and panko to the leftovers, baked it, and served it with a pile of cracklin' pork skins as an appetizer for girls' night. It was another hit. This recipe helps you use those delicious, but sometimes overabundant, collards twice and I just love a two-for-one special!

Conecuh Collards
—— **4 TO 6 SERVINGS**

2 lb [900 g] collard greens

4 cups [960 ml] chicken stock or broth

3 Tbsp unsalted butter

2 dried whole chile peppers

3 cups [675 g] finely chopped Conecuh sausage

3 cups [450 g] thinly sliced onion

¼ cup [60 ml] apple cider vinegar

3 garlic cloves, thinly sliced

Pinch of red pepper flakes

Prepare the collards by slicing down the sides of the stalks to remove the leafy greens. Chiffonade the leaves and dice the stalks. Keep them separate. Place the collard leaves and chicken stock in a medium Dutch oven over medium-high heat. Bring to a boil, then simmer for 30 minutes. Drain the leaves in a colander.

In a medium-large cast iron skillet over medium heat, melt the butter, then add the peppers and sausage. Cook, stirring frequently, for 10 to 12 minutes, or until the fat has rendered and the sausage is brown. Remove the sausage and peppers, leaving the fat in the skillet.

cont'd

109

Add the diced collard stalks and the onion and cook for 20 minutes over low heat, stirring frequently, until the onions are mostly caramelized. Turn the heat to medium-high, add the vinegar, garlic, and red pepper flakes, and cook for 5 minutes, or until the liquid is evaporated. Add the sausage, peppers, and cooked collard greens to the skillet. Cook over low heat for 20 to 30 minutes, or until the liquid is evaporated and the greens are dark in color. Serve hot.

Alabama "Spinach" Dip
—— 4 TO 6 SERVINGS

2 cups [220 g] freshly grated Parmesan cheese

½ cup [120 g] mayonnaise

1 recipe Conecuh Collards (page 109)

1 cup [100 g] freshly grated aged Gouda cheese

1 cup [100 g] panko bread crumbs

2 Tbsp unsalted butter, melted, plus more for greasing the dish

¼ cup [30 g] fine ground cornmeal, for dusting the dish

Pork skins, tortilla chips, or pita chips, for serving

Preheat the oven to 350°F [175°C]. In a large mixing bowl, fold the Parmesan and mayonnaise into the Conecuh Collards. In a medium mixing bowl, toss together the Gouda, panko, and butter. Grease an 11 by 7 in [28 by 18 cm] (2 qt [1.9 ml]) casserole dish and dust with the cornmeal. Pour the collard mixture into the dish, then top with the panko mixture. Bake for 20 to 30 minutes, or until golden brown on top, bubbling, and brown on the edges. Serve hot with pork skins, tortilla chips, or pita chips.

Pepper Jelly Brussels Sprouts

4 TO 6 SERVINGS

When I first put Brussels sprouts on my menu, my staff wouldn't even try them. They all thought I was crazy or, worse, out to get them. "You'll never get anyone in this town to eat those nasty things!" they said. And, "I'm not trying 'em—I don't care if you're my boss or not!" I kept my mouth shut. You see, I'd worked with these babies for months at Café Boulud, and we had an understanding. I cut them in half, tossed them with olive oil and salt, and roasted them to golden. Then I plopped them in the fryer, crisping up the leaves like potato chips until they were a dark olive brown. I immediately tossed them in pepper jelly, sprinkled them with Parmesan dust, and placed them in front of my staff. I converted each of 'em to Brussels-lovers, and the love has grown. These sprouts are now more popular than our nachos.

5 cups [700 g] fresh Brussels sprouts, halved vertically

½ cup [120 ml] olive oil

1 Tbsp salt

Canola oil, for frying

½ cup [170 g] Pepper Jelly (page 58)

¼ cup [28 g] finely grated Parmesan (almost dust consistency)

Preheat the oven to 400°F [205°C]. Line a sheet pan with parchment paper. In a large mixing bowl, toss together the sprouts, olive oil, and salt. Roast on the prepared pan for 15 minutes or until golden.

In a medium cast iron skillet, pour the canola oil to 2 to 3 in [5 to 8 cm] deep. Heat the oil to 350°F [175°C]. Line a plate with paper towels. Place 10 to 15 sprouts in the oil and step back; they will pop and bubble. Fry until they have stopped bubbling and are super crispy, about 5 to 7 minutes. Using a slotted spoon, transfer the sprouts to the paper towels to drain, then toss with the Pepper Jelly in a medium mixing bowl. While hot, sprinkle with the Parmesan and serve.

No. 3

Potatoe[s]

& P[

Grains
Pasta

Papa Karl's German Potato Salad

4 TO 6 SERVINGS

When my great-great-grandparents immigrated from Germany over one hundred years ago, they arrived in Mobile, Alabama, and opened their family restaurant, Karl's Café. They served wholesome comfort food with German and Southern Gulf influences. They were famous for this delicious potato salad.

5 lb [2.3 kg] new potatoes, quartered

2 Tbsp salt, plus more to taste

1 cup [240 ml] canola oil

½ cup [120 ml] apple cider vinegar

3 Tbsp mayonnaise

3 Tbsp stone ground mustard

2 Tbsp freshly ground black pepper

1 Tbsp horseradish

1 tsp celery seed

1 tsp garlic powder

1 cup [150 g] chopped green onions

½ cup [15 g] chopped fresh parsley

¼ cup [5 g] chopped fresh dill

Place the potatoes and salt in a large pot and cover with cold water so that all the potatoes are submerged. Over high heat, bring the water to a boil, then lower the heat and simmer for 10 to 15 minutes, until the potatoes are barely tender when pierced with a knife. Drain the potatoes in a colander, then place the colander with the potatoes over the empty pot and cover with a clean, dry kitchen towel. Allow the potatoes to steam and drain for 15 to 20 minutes.

In a large mixing bowl, whisk together the oil, vinegar, mayonnaise, mustard, pepper, horseradish, celery seed, and garlic powder. Fold in the onions, parsley, and dill. Season with salt and set aside.

While the potatoes are still warm, toss them in a large bowl with the dressing to coat, then cover and refrigerate for at least 1 hour. Season with salt. Serve cold or at room temperature. Refrigerate in an airtight container for up to 3 days.

Smashed Crispy Potatoes

3 TO 4 SERVINGS

I am a huge fan of butter, but I'm also a really big fan of my pants fitting. Therefore, I often cook lighter meals during the week, saving my richer recipes for the weekend. These potatoes are a weekday recipe that I often serve with plain Greek yogurt and green onions for a mock twice-baked potato. Or, served with ketchup, the kids think they are french fries!

1½ lb [680 g] whole petite red potatoes

¼ cup [60 ml] olive oil

1 Tbsp salt

1 Tbsp garlic powder

1 Tbsp onion powder

8 to 10 turns freshly ground black pepper

Preheat the oven to 400°F [205°C]. Line a sheet pan with foil or parchment paper.

In a large mixing bowl, toss the potatoes with the olive oil, salt, and garlic and onion powders. Place the potatoes on the prepared pan. Roast, stirring occasionally, for 20 to 30 minutes, or until they are easily pierced with a fork. Remove from the oven and smash the potatoes lightly with the back of a spoon.

Increase the heat to 450°F [230°C] and cook the smashed potatoes for an additional 10 to 15 minutes, or until crispy and deep golden on top. Remove from the oven and top with the black pepper. Enjoy immediately or refrigerate in an airtight container for up to 3 days.

Sweetie's Thanksgiving Casserole

My great-grandmother Sweetie made this every year, and we have all carried on the tradition. It is without a doubt the best version of this dish I've tasted. It actually tastes of sweet potatoes and is speckled with orange throughout—a refreshing contrast to the typical oversugared, overmixed, and overly processed versions that the South most frequently dotes on. It is a dish that, as a chef, I frequently have admired for its flavor balance and "outside the box" preparation.

···· **NOTE** ····

Make ahead by preparing the casserole, covering with foil, and refrigerating for up to 3 days. Let sit at room temperature for 30 minutes or up to an hour before baking.

8 medium (about 4 lb [1.8 kg]) sweet potatoes, peeled, cubed large

1 cup [170 g] packed light brown sugar

2 tsp cinnamon

2 tsp nutmeg

2 tsp salt

1 large orange

½ cup [115 g] unsalted butter, melted, plus more for buttering the dish

2 cups [200 g] pecans, toasted and chopped

2 cups [250 g] miniature marshmallows

Preheat the oven to 350°F [175°C]. Butter a 9 by 13 in [23 by 33 cm] pan and set aside.

Place the sweet potatoes in a large pot and fill with water to cover. Bring to a boil over medium-high heat, then turn down to a simmer and cook until tender when pierced with a fork, 15 to 20 minutes. Drain the potatoes in a colander in the sink and let cool.

In a small bowl, combine the sugar, cinnamon, nutmeg, and salt.

In a separate small bowl, combine the orange zest, juice, and some of the pulp. Add the melted butter and stir to combine.

In the prepared pan, lay out half of the sweet potato chunks, sprinkle with half of the sugar mixture, drizzle with half of the orange/butter mixture, scatter with half of the pecans, and repeat to create two layers. Top with the marshmallows.

Bake for 20 to 30 minutes, or until the marshmallows are golden and the casserole is bubbling around the edges. Serve hot.

Sorghum and Pecan Sweet Potatoes

3 TO 4 SERVINGS

This trio of quintessentially Southern ingredients makes my heart flutter. Sweet potatoes are such a perfect food on their own, and the simple garnishes added here enhance their flavor without smothering them. This simple, wholesome side is a favorite at our house.

4 medium sweet potatoes (about 2 lb [900 g]), peeled, cubed large

½ cup [115 g] unsalted butter, melted

½ cup [120 ml] sorghum syrup

2 tsp salt, plus more to taste

½ tsp cinnamon

½ tsp nutmeg

1 cup [100 g] coarsely chopped pecans, toasted

Zest and juice of 1 lemon

Preheat the oven to 400°F [205°C]. Line a half sheet pan with parchment paper.

In a large mixing bowl, toss together the sweet potatoes, melted butter, sorghum syrup, salt, cinnamon, and nutmeg until the potatoes are coated. Roast, stirring three or four times, for 30 to 45 minutes, or until the potatoes are tender when pierced with a fork and have taken on a brown caramel color. Toss with the toasted pecans and lemon zest and juice, then season with salt. Serve hot.

Smoked Gouda Grits with Redeye Gravy

4 TO 6 SERVINGS

Grits are my ramen and my mac and cheese. I grew up eating them with fried eggs every single morning, and now, if I am not feeling so hot or need some extra comfort, they are my go-to. I speak with conviction when saying that you can put just about anything in a bowl with grits and total satisfaction will result. This combination, however, might be my absolute favorite.

I was testing gravy recipes for the brunch menu at KBC. As I often do when I recipe test, I was only tasting components and hadn't actually eaten anything of substance. A few hours in, I was starving and looking for a quick fix. I scooped a heaping mound of our smoked Gouda grits into a bowl and poured the nearest thing over it, which happened to be redeye gravy. I was immediately satiated by the flavorful combination and left in a buttery euphoria. It's my best accidental recipe to date.

FOR THE SMOKED GOUDA GRITS

3 cups [720 ml] whole milk

5 Tbsp [70 g] unsalted butter

Salt

1 cup [165 g] stone ground yellow grits

1½ cups [150 g] grated smoked Gouda

2 Tbsp cream

FOR THE REDEYE GRAVY

5 Tbsp [70 g] unsalted butter

¼ cup [30 g] all-purpose flour

4 cups [960 ml] beef broth

½ cup [120 ml] freshly brewed coffee, hot

1 tsp soy sauce

1 tsp black pepper

To make the grits: In a medium saucepan over medium heat, bring the milk to a simmer with 4 Tbsp [58 g] of the butter, then add a dash of salt. Slowly whisk in the grits. Lower the heat to low and cook, whisking frequently, for 20 minutes, or until the grits are tender and creamy. Remove from the heat, whisk in the remaining 1 Tbsp of butter, the Gouda, and cream, and season with salt. Serve immediately or cover with foil and place in the oven at 300°F [150°C] until ready to serve.

To make the gravy: In a medium saucepan over medium heat, melt 4 Tbsp [58 g] of the butter, then whisk in the flour to form a blonde roux. Pour in the broth and coffee and bring to a boil, whisking constantly. Lower the heat to low and simmer for 15 to 20 minutes, or until the sauce has a gravy consistency. Remove from the heat and whisk in the remaining butter, the soy sauce, and black pepper. Serve immediately over hot grits.

Baked Cheese Grits

10 TO 12 SERVINGS

In the South, we like to find any excuse to eat grits. Baked grits are most often seen at potlucks or brunches and also make regular appearances as supper side dishes. They're known for the distinct Cheddar addition as well as their casserole-like texture.

6 cups [1.4 L] chicken broth or stock

1 tsp salt, plus more to taste

2 cups [330 g] stone ground yellow grits

2 cups [200 g] freshly grated extra sharp Cheddar

1 cup [30 g] freshly grated Parmesan cheese

½ cup [120 ml] whole milk

¼ tsp garlic powder

4 eggs, beaten

½ cup [115 g] unsalted butter, plus more for greasing the dish

Preheat the oven to 350°F [175°C]. Grease a 4 qt [3.8 L] casserole dish and set aside.

In a medium saucepan over medium-high heat, bring the broth to a boil, then add the salt. Slowly whisk in the grits, then lower the heat to low and cook, whisking frequently, until the grits are thick, 8 to 10 minutes. Add 1 cup [100 g] of the Cheddar, the Parmesan, milk, and garlic powder, then stir to completely incorporate. Slowly whisk in the eggs and butter, stirring until completely combined. Season with salt.

Pour the mixture into the prepared casserole dish and top with the remaining 1 cup [100 g] of Cheddar. Bake for 30 to 45 minutes, or until bubbling and set. Serve immediately or keep warm in the oven, covered, at 275°F [135°C] until ready to serve. If you plan to enjoy it later, refrigerate in an airtight container for up to 3 days.

Baked Corn Grits

These grits are an echo of a soufflé, thanks to the eggs, and the sweetness of the corn rounds out the flavors of this dish. These pair perfectly with Creole Tomato Gravy Shrimp (page 151).

6 cups [1.4 L] chicken broth

1 tsp salt

2 cups [330 g] stone ground yellow grits

One 15.25 oz [450 ml] can creamed corn

2 cups [220 g] freshly grated Parmesan cheese

½ cup [120 ml] whole milk

¼ tsp garlic powder

4 eggs, beaten

½ cup [115 g] unsalted butter

Preheat the oven to 350°F [175°C]. Grease a 4 qt [3.8 L] casserole dish and set aside.

In a medium saucepan over medium-high heat, bring the broth to a boil, then add the salt. Slowly whisk in the grits and corn, then lower the heat to low and cook, whisking frequently, for 8 to 10 minutes, or until the grits are thick. Add 1 cup [110 g] of the Parmesan cheese, the milk, and the garlic powder and stir to completely incorporate. Slowly whisk in the eggs and butter, stirring until completely combined.

Pour the mixture into the prepared casserole dish and top with the remaining Parmesan cheese. Bake for 30 to 45 minutes, or until bubbling and set, then cool for 20 to 30 minutes before serving. Serve immediately or keep warm in the oven, covered, at 275°F [135°C] until ready to serve. If you plan to enjoy it later, refrigerate in an airtight container for up to 3 days.

Dirty Rice

4 TO 6 SERVINGS

I am a huge fan of Cajun food, and this recipe is one I've always been fond of. It was traditionally made with leftover meat—frugality being a shared trait of Southern and Cajun food. In my opinion, however, you can't make dirty rice without livers. So if you're wondering what to substitute for them, the answer is nothing. Give this one a try; it may surprise you!

2 Tbsp unsalted butter

1 lb [450 g] ground pork sausage

1 lb [450 g] chicken livers, rinsed in cold water, finely chopped

1 cup [150 g] chopped onion

1 cup [150 g] chopped celery

1 cup [150 g] chopped bell pepper

1 tsp salt, plus more for seasoning

2 garlic cloves, chopped

¼ cup [60 ml] apple cider vinegar

2 Tbsp tomato paste

1 cup [180 g] long-grain rice (I like Carolina Gold for this)

1 tsp cayenne pepper

2 cups [480 ml] chicken stock or broth

¼ cup [5 g] chopped fresh parsley (optional)

Crystal hot sauce (optional)

In a large cast iron skillet or medium Dutch oven over medium heat, melt the butter. Add the sausage and livers and fry for 4 to 5 minutes, or until brown and cooked through. Remove the sausage and livers from the skillet, leaving the fat behind. Lower the heat to medium-low and add the onion, celery, bell peppers, and salt. Cook for 5 to 6 minutes, or until slightly caramelized and translucent. Add the garlic and cook, stirring frequently, for 2 to 3 more minutes. Add the apple cider vinegar and tomato paste and cook for 2 to 3 minutes, or until the liquid has almost completely reduced.

Add the pork, livers, rice, and cayenne and stir lightly to combine. Add the stock and bring to a boil. Cover the skillet and cook over very low heat for exactly 15 minutes. Remove the skillet from the heat and let the rice stand, covered, for 5 minutes.

Fluff the rice with a fork, season with salt, garnish with parsley and hot sauce, if using, and serve.

126

Butter Bean Hoppin' John with Cilantro-Lime Vinaigrette

4 TO 6 SERVINGS

There are many stories about where Hoppin' John got its name, but one thing is unanimous around the Southern table: it's not Hoppin' John unless there's pork, peas, and rice. It's traditionally a one-pot meal, but I prefer to cook the peas separately to be sure they're not overdone, and I use lima beans instead of traditional black-eyed peas. You may have to wash another pot, but it's worth the extra step.

5 cups [1.2 L] chicken stock or broth

3 cups [435 g] baby butter beans, fresh or frozen

6 slices thick-cut bacon

1½ cups [225 g] chopped onion

1 cup [150 g] chopped celery

1 cup [150 g] chopped green bell pepper

2 garlic cloves, chopped

1 cup [180 g] long grain rice (I like Carolina Gold for this)

½ tsp cayenne pepper

½ tsp freshly ground black pepper

Salt

Cilantro-Lime Vinaigrette (recipe follows)

¼ cup [5 g] chopped fresh parsley

¼ cup [35 g] chopped green onions

In a medium saucepot over medium heat, bring 3 cups [720 ml] of the chicken stock, the beans, and 1 slice of the bacon to a slow simmer. Cook for 15 to 20 minutes, or until tender. Blanch by straining the peas and submerging them in ice-cold water to rapidly cool down. Let the beans sit for 10 minutes, or until cool throughout, then drain and place on paper towels to absorb excess liquid. Set aside.

cont'd

129

Chop the remaining 5 bacon slices and place them in a medium Dutch oven over medium-low heat. Cook, stirring frequently, for 8 to 10 minutes, or until the bacon just starts to crisp. Add the onion, celery, bell pepper, and garlic and continue to cook until tender and slightly translucent, 8 to 10 more minutes. Add the rice, cayenne, and black pepper to the pot and stir gently to combine. Add the remaining 2 cups [480 ml] of chicken stock and bring to a boil. Cover the Dutch oven and cook the rice over very low heat for exactly 15 minutes. Remove the pan from the heat and let the rice stand, covered, for 5 minutes. Meanwhile, prepare the Cilantro-Lime Vinaigrette.

Fluff the rice with a fork, then gently fold in the cooked butter beans and season with salt. To serve, drizzle individual portions with Cilantro-Lime Vinaigrette and garnish with the parsley and green onions.

Cilantro-Lime Vinaigrette

½ cup [120 ml] extra-virgin olive oil

½ cup [10 g] chopped cilantro, packed

¼ cup [35 g] chopped onion

3 Tbsp freshly squeezed lime juice

2 garlic cloves

1 tsp salt

Combine all the ingredients in a food processor and purée until smooth. Serve immediately or refrigerate in an airtight container for up to 1 week.

Potlikker Field Pea Risotto

This recipe is a happy accident that came about when I was prepping for a small dinner at the Aspen Food and Wine Festival. It was a private, invite-only dinner for thirty people. Our prep area was a pop-up tent with two propane burners, pots, pans, and an open fire. Ironically, this is where I do my best, most thoughtful cooking. My intention was to cook the field peas, purée them, then fold them into the already cooked risotto. We also had limited water, which is where the idea came about. I cooked the peas, reserved the water, and cooked the risotto in the potlikker water—and behold, this dish was born.

7 Tbsp [98 g] unsalted butter

10 cups [2.4 L] chicken stock or broth

2 cups [290 g] lady peas, fresh or frozen (thaw before using)

Salt

5 Tbsp [75 ml] olive oil

1½ cups [225 g] finely chopped onion

2 cups [390 g] Arborio rice

1 cup [240 ml] dry white wine

2 cups [220 g] finely grated Parmesan cheese

In a 6 qt [5.7 L] Dutch oven over medium-high heat, melt 2 Tbsp of the butter, then add the stock, peas, and 1 Tbsp of salt. Bring to a boil, then turn down to a low simmer. Cover and cook for 20 minutes, or until just tender. Do not let the peas crack and become mush—this happens when the peas are cooked over too high heat, causing them to burst, or when they are cooked for too long. Drain the peas in a colander over a medium pot, then set the peas aside. Place the pot with the reserved pea stock on a burner over very low heat to keep it hot.

cont'd

131

Add the oil and onion to the Dutch oven and cook over medium heat, stirring frequently with a wooden spoon, until the onions are translucent and have started to soften, 6 to 8 minutes. Add the rice and cook, stirring constantly, for about 5 minutes. Add the wine and a pinch of salt, then bring to a simmer over medium-high heat until the wine is completely evaporated, 2 to 3 minutes.

Lower the heat to medium-low, then add the hot pea stock to the rice in 1 cup [240 ml] increments, stirring constantly and allowing the liquid to fully absorb before adding more, until the rice is al dente (still chewy) and surrounded by liquid. Each addition should take 2 to 3 minutes to be absorbed, with a total cooking time of 20 to 30 minutes. The final product should be loose, creamy, and cooked throughout.

Remove from the heat, then stir in the remaining 5 Tbsp [70 g] of butter, 1 cup [110 g] of the Parmesan, and the field peas and season with salt. Serve immediately, sprinkled with the remaining Parmesan.

◼ NOTE ◼

This is a "toddler recipe." You cannot leave it unattended. The key to great risotto is allowing the rice to slowly absorb the liquid while constantly moving it, encouraging the starches to release from the rice, creating its characteristic silky consistency. Prepare to stand and stir continuously for the full thirtyish minutes it takes to prepare. The more love you show it, the more you receive.

No. 4

Sea

good

Oyster Bar with Cocktail Sauce

6 SERVINGS

There is a hole-in-the-wall oyster bar in every respectable Southern town within thirty miles of the coast, and they are all pretty similar. There's a bar that anyone can shimmy up to, but those seats are tacitly reserved for daily regulars. On any given Saturday you might end up sharing a table with your preacher, hairdresser, therapist, or kindergarten teacher over lunch. You order beer—ice-cold American longnecks. Don't even think about asking for anything else. You order your oysters raw or baked, and if you're really feelin' fancy, you add on a chili dog. You ask for saltines, Crystal hot sauce, and of course, cocktail sauce. I like my cocktail sauce packing heat and more flavorful than what you'll find on the shelf. This recipe always delivers.

2 cups [520 g] ketchup

1 Tbsp stone ground mustard

1 Tbsp freshly grated horseradish

1 Tbsp Crystal hot sauce

1 tsp onion powder

1 tsp Worcestershire sauce

1 dozen raw briny oysters, shucked

12 saltine crackers

In a mixing bowl, whisk together the ketchup, mustard, horseradish, hot sauce, onion powder, and Worcestershire. Enjoy immediately or keep refrigerated in a tightly sealed container for up to 1 month.

To serve, place the oysters in a pan over ice, with crackers and sauce on the side. To eat, place an oyster on a cracker and spoon cocktail sauce over the top.

Garden Pepper Jelly Mignonette

6 SERVINGS

A lot of things shock you when you move from the South to the North, or vice versa. Up North, people talk funny, move faster, and don't wave to strangers on the street. But, as I discovered, the North also offers an insanely delicious oyster experience.

It was January when I moved to New York City, and shortly after I arrived, a massive blizzard hit. When I emerged after four days of being stuck inside, trying to convince myself this move hadn't been a huge mistake, I had to find me some oysters—I needed that immediate connection to home.

I snuck into the first oyster bar I spotted with a sign that read "Happy hour special, $1 a dozen!" A DOLLAR a DOZEN! I sat down on a clean, vintage seat and rested my hands on a white marble table. I ordered a glass of champagne and a dozen raw oysters, feeling pretty cheeky. My order arrived sans cocktail sauce, saltines, or hot sauce; rather, with mignonette sauce. I topped each oyster with mignonette, gulped the first one down, and took a sip of champagne. The bubbles electrified this perfect little bite and sent fireworks of refreshing, salty goodness over my taste buds. So this is what I'd been missing out on? I love my Southern traditions, but that combo kicked it out of the water.

Here's my own take on the mignonette to remind me of those New York days. Pepper jelly is typically made at the end of the summer when you've done just about everything you can with your garden peppers and it's time to start canning. It's most familiar on top of braised collards, but it can be used for so much more.

2 cups [480 ml] Pepper Jelly (page 58) or store-bought

1 Tbsp minced red onion

1 Tbsp coarsely ground black pepper

1 dozen raw briny oysters, shucked

In a mixing bowl, combine the pepper jelly, red onion, and pepper. Let sit for 30 minutes to 1 hour in the refrigerator or for 1 to 2 hours at room temperature before use.

To serve, place the oysters in a pan over ice, then top each one with 1 Tbsp of the pepper jelly mix. Serve immediately.

Alabama Oysters

6 SERVINGS

When we were asked to cater a boat party on *Top Chef*, my first thought was oysters. This is the recipe I turned to, as it marries classic Northern and Southern preparations. The flavors of cocktail sauce and hot sauce satisfy my Southern taste buds, while the preparation recalls a Northern mignonette. It's a surprising, refreshing twist on both classics.

✦ NOTE ✦

I serve raw oysters for large parties at my home and for catering events quite often, so I came up with this hostess hack. Shuck all your oysters ahead of time, save the liquid from the shells, place the oyster bodies in this liquid in a sealed container, and refrigerate. Rinse the shells in the sink to remove dirt, then place in the dishwasher. Run the dishwasher on hot with no soap. The steam gets the shells shiny and clean with no scrubbing needed. Place the shells in the freezer or a cooler with ice. Just before the party starts, lay the shells out on a tray with ice and plop the reserved oyster bodies back into them, discarding excess liquid. No muss, no fuss, and the coldest oysters you've ever had.

COCKTAIL SAUCE NAGE

2 cups [480 ml] tomato purée

¼ cup [31 g] freshly grated horseradish

Zest and juice of 1 lemon

1 tsp Worcestershire sauce

¼ tsp soy sauce

GARNISH

¼ cup [60 ml] red wine vinegar

2 Tbsp finely diced cucumber

2 Tbsp finely diced red onion

2 Tbsp finely diced celery

2 tsp coarsely ground black pepper

1 tsp salt

1 dozen raw briny oysters, shucked

To make the nage: In a small saucepan over medium-high heat, combine the tomato purée, horseradish, lemon zest and juice, Worcestershire, and soy sauce. Bring to a boil, then remove from the heat and let cool to room temperature, 20 minutes. Strain the mixture through a cheesecloth until it is completely smooth, then place in an airtight container in the refrigerator for at least 1 hour. Keep refrigerated until ready to serve; it should be ice cold. The nage will keep refrigerated in an airtight container for up to 1 week.

To make the garnish: In a small bowl, toss together all the ingredients. Let stand at room temperature for 10 to 15 minutes or up to 1 hour.

To serve: Place the oysters in a pan over ice and top each with 1 Tbsp of the nage, then 1 tsp of the garnish mixture. Serve immediately.

Marinated Crab Claws

4 TO 6 SERVINGS

I created this recipe for KBC when we decided to expand to serve supper. I wanted a seafood-heavy menu with Southern dishes that were elevated but reminiscent of beloved staples. Crab claws are everywhere in the South, and they are always served in one of two ways: cornmeal fried with a side of tartar sauce or swimming in a bowl of gumbo. These Marinated Crab Claws are a bright, fresh twist that brings out the natural sweet flavor of the crab. They are deceptively easy to prepare and are completely addictive. I typically serve them with a piece of grilled bread to dip in the leftover marinade.

½ cup [120 ml] olive oil

¼ cup [25 g] chopped green onions

2 Tbsp minced red onion

2 Tbsp chopped fresh parsley

2 Tbsp chopped fresh dill

2 Tbsp red wine vinegar

1 Tbsp freshly ground black pepper

1 tsp Worcestershire sauce

½ tsp celery salt

½ tsp salt

6 to 8 drops Crystal hot sauce

¼ tsp freshly ground horseradish

1 lb [450 g] cooked blue crab claws, outer shells removed

In a large mixing bowl, combine all the ingredients except the crab claws and whisk to mix well. Add the crab claws and toss to coat. Cover and refrigerate for at least 4 hours or overnight.

Serve chilled or at cool room temperature. The claws will keep refrigerated in an airtight container for up to 2 days.

Grandmama's West Indies Crab Salad

4 TO 6 SERVINGS

West Indies salad is old-school Southern and was my grandmother's favorite dish to bring to a party. There was magic in her ice-cold glass bowl of seafood delicacy. We'd often serve this as an appetizer before our fish fries, fighting over it and scooping up every morsel as fast as we could. Keep it simple by serving with classic saltine crackers. You know what they say: Don't mess with perfection.

½ cup [75 g] minced onion

½ cup [120 ml] canola oil

¼ cup [60 ml] apple cider vinegar

1 tsp salt

1 tsp freshly ground black pepper

1 lb [450 g] cooked jumbo lump crabmeat

Combine the onion, oil, vinegar, salt, and pepper in a large mixing bowl and whisk to mix well. Add the crab and toss to coat. Cover and refrigerate for at least 1 hour or overnight.

Serve chilled or at cool room temperature. The salad will keep refrigerated in an airtight container for up to 2 days.

Grandmother Lil's Crab Omelet Sandwiches

4 TO 6 SERVINGS

This recipe is my family's most prized possession. It originated with my Great-Grandmother Lil who passed the torch down to my Grandmother June, who passed it to my aunts and mom, who passed it to me, my siblings, and cousins. The family recipe is purposefully vague—it's dependent on being taught by a family member. We make these on special occasions, and even had a crab omelet station at my Grandmother June's funeral. I've never seen a similar recipe, and feel a sense of pride knowing my great-grandmother created this dish on her own merit. Welcome to the family!

12 eggs, separated

1 lb [450 g] fresh jumbo lump crabmeat

1 cup [25 g] chopped fresh parsley

1 tsp salt, plus more to taste

1 tsp freshly ground black pepper, plus more to taste

½ cup [120 g] mayonnaise

1 loaf Wonder white bread

3 large ripe tomatoes, sliced ¼ in [6 mm] thick

In a large mixing bowl, whisk the egg yolks, then stir in the crab, parsley, salt, and pepper, until completely coated in egg yolk. Set aside.

In a stand mixer with the whisk attachment, whisk the egg whites on medium-high speed until they form stiff peaks. Fold the egg whites into the yolk mixture in three additions until completely combined.

To cook, place 4 to 6 oz [115 to 170 g] of the mixture in a greased griddle or skillet over medium-low heat. The mixture should resemble a pancake in size and shape. Let the omelet slightly brown on the edges, about 2 minutes, then flip and cook on the other side for 2 more minutes, or until cooked throughout and very light golden. Repeat with the remaining batter.

To assemble each sandwich, spread 1 Tbsp of the mayonnaise on two slices of white bread, add two slices of tomato, then sprinkle with salt and pepper. Add one omelet and cut the sandwich in half. Serve immediately.

Po'Boys
with Remoulade

4 SERVINGS

As a child, I looked forward to so much about our annual trips to New Orleans, but top of the list were beignets and po'boys. I still love these so much that I added them to the supper menu at KBC. Soft-shell crab and oyster po'boys are my favorite, but I've got to be honest with y'all, you can sandwich just about any fresh seafood between rolls topped with my remoulade and it will be an instant hit. My only advice for choosing is to go with what looks freshest when visiting your local fish market—or, better yet, go with what you catch!

3 cups [720 ml] buttermilk

½ cup [120 ml] pickle juice

Crystal hot sauce

SEAFOOD OF CHOICE (YOU ONLY NEED ONE OF THE FOLLOWING)

1½ lb [680 g] fresh shrimp, peeled and deveined

2 dozen raw oysters, freshly shucked

4 softshell crabs

Four 6 to 8 oz [170 to 225 g] fillets of catfish, snapper, grouper, or similar flaky white fish

4 cups [960 ml] canola oil, for frying

1 cup [125 g] all-purpose flour

1 cup [130 g] fine ground cornmeal

1 Tbsp garlic powder

½ Tbsp onion powder

½ Tbsp celery salt

½ tsp freshly ground black pepper

½ tsp cayenne pepper

Salt

Four 8 in [20 cm] long French rolls, fresh and crusty, split horizontally

3 medium tomatoes, sliced into ¼ in [6 mm] rounds

3 cups [75 g] freshly shredded iceberg lettuce

1 cup [240 g] Remoulade (recipe follows)

¼ cup [35 g] sliced green onion

¼ cup [5 g] chopped parsley

1 lemon, cut into wedges

In a large bowl or deep casserole dish, combine the buttermilk, pickle juice, and 6 to 8 dashes of hot sauce. Brine the seafood in the mixture for at least 1 hour or up to overnight.

cont'd

Fill a deep pot or fryer halfway with oil and heat to 350°F [175°C]. Set a cooling rack on a sheet pan or line a plate with paper towels. In a medium bowl, stir together the flour, cornmeal, garlic and onion powders, celery salt, black pepper, and cayenne until combined. Dredge all the seafood pieces, following the dredging instructions in Bee's Fried Chicken (see page 181).

Deep fry the seafood for 7 to 8 minutes, or until golden brown and crispy. Place on the prepared rack or paper towels to absorb excess oil. Sprinkle with salt.

Assemble the sandwiches by lining the rolls with the tomatoes, then adding the seafood and topping with the lettuce and a drizzle of the remoulade. Garnish with the green onions, parsley, and more hot sauce. Squeeze a lemon wedge over the top of each sandwich and enjoy immediately.

Remoulade
—— 2 CUPS [620 G]

1 cup [240 g] mayonnaise

½ cup [120 g] sour cream

½ cup [120 ml] buttermilk

¼ cup [35 g] chopped onion

¼ cup [35 g] chopped celery

2 garlic cloves

2 Tbsp ketchup

2 Tbsp fresh parsley

2 Tbsp black pepper

1 Tbsp salt

1 tsp red wine vinegar

¼ tsp horseradish

6 to 8 dashes hot sauce

Combine all the ingredients in a food processor. Process until completely smooth. Taste and adjust the seasoning. Enjoy immediately or keep refrigerated in an airtight container for up to 3 weeks.

Sweetie's Gumbo

The smell of roux reminds me of my childhood. In the spring, as soon as the chill left the air, our family would head to our beach house on the Gulf. On the way, we'd stop to get chicken thighs and fish carcasses at the grocery store—we couldn't miss an hour of catching time.

I learned how to avoid biting crab claws before I could tie my shoes properly and mastered the art of cleaning them before I could braid my hair. We'd bring the cleaned crabs up from the dock and dump them right into the pot. My mom's dark roux would have been simmering all day in the skillet, and that rich smell would taunt us until we could hardly stand it. Once the crabs were just done enough, we'd sit around our newspaper-covered table to crack and dig out the precious, sweet meat until there wasn't a drop of it left. It was always silent once the crabs hit the table—a miracle in our family.

It wasn't until I was older that I realized how unique this tradition was. Gumbo, jambalaya, and red beans and rice were repeat dishes in my family. My Mobile, Alabama, grandmothers and great-grandmothers added a unique twist of Cajun flavors and an attitude we wouldn't have been exposed to otherwise. These women weren't afraid to do the dirty work and, in fact, relished the opportunity.

Every time I whisk roux in my grandmother's cast iron skillet, I can't help but acknowledge the similarities between its traits and the matriarchs of my family. To develop properly, it requires patience and careful attention. Strong, classic, steady, and the binder that holds everything together. It's of the utmost importance and leaves a lasting impression.

SHELLFISH STOCK

1 lb [450 g] shell-on, raw, medium fresh shrimp (ideally from the Gulf)

1 bunch parsley stems (reserve the leaves for garnish)

1 bunch whole green onion bulbs (reserve the green tops for garnish)

2 sprigs thyme

3 bay leaves

2 Tbsp black peppercorns

GUMBO SAUCE

1½ cups [345 g] unsalted butter, melted

2½ cups [315 g] all-purpose flour

2 cups [300 g] chopped onion

2 stalks celery, chopped

1 cup [150 g] chopped bell pepper

12 oz [340 g] andouille sausage, sliced into ⅓ in [8 mm] rounds

2 cups [300 g] chopped fresh okra, sliced ¼ in [6 mm] thick

6 garlic cloves, minced

One 28 oz [790 g] can crushed tomatoes

8 to 12 cups [2 to 2.9 L] Shellfish Stock

2 bay leaves

1 Tbsp filé powder (can substitute with 4 bay leaves)

1 tsp cayenne powder

Salt

2 lb [900 g] fresh blue crab (whole), fresh crab claws, or 1 lb [450 g] container jumbo lump crabmeat

6 cups [1 kg] cooked basmati rice, for serving

1 cup [20 g] chopped parsley, for garnish

1 cup [100 g] chopped green onion, for garnish

Crystal or Tabasco hot sauce, for garnish

1 cup [150 g] oyster crackers, for garnish

cont'd

To make the shellfish stock: Peel the shrimp by pulling off the legs, then pinching the tails (save the shells). Refrigerate the peeled shrimp separately in a bowl covered tightly in plastic wrap. Place the shrimp shells in a 14 to 20 qt [13 to 19 L] stockpot. Toast over high heat, stirring consistently until they turn pink in color, 2 to 3 minutes. Add 3 qt [2.8 L] of water and the parsley stems, green onion bulbs, thyme, bay leaves, and black peppercorns. Bring the stock to a boil, then immediately turn down to a simmer. Continue to simmer while preparing the rest of the meal.

To make the gumbo sauce: In a large Dutch oven over medium-low heat, melt the butter, then slowly whisk in the flour. Cook the roux for about 15 minutes, whisking constantly, until it is dark brown, the color of a milk chocolate bar. Turn down the heat to low, then add the onion, celery, bell pepper, and sausage and cook, stirring constantly with a wooden spoon, for 10 more minutes, or until it is a deep, dark brown color. Add the okra, garlic, and tomatoes and cook for 5 more minutes.

Using a large ladle, slowly add the stock, letting it incorporate after each addition. Continue adding stock until the gumbo reaches a nappe consistency (see page 37). Add the bay leaves, filé, and cayenne and season with salt. Simmer over low heat for at least 30 minutes or up to 6 hours. Add the crab and the reserved shrimp and simmer for 20 minutes. Refrigerate for up to 4 days in a sealed container and warm before serving over rice, garnishing with parsley, green onions, hot sauce, and crackers.

Pro tip: Always make this the day before you intend to serve it. The cooling and reheating process is what really enhances the flavors of the stew. The best way to reheat gumbo—or any thick stew—is to place it in a double boiler and let it slowly warm. This prevents any burning or sticking on the bottom of the pot. Hostess bonus: While your gumbo warms, you have all the time you need to get yourself and your home guest-ready.

★ NOTE ★

BEST CASE
Make shellfish stock as directed.

HACK
Shortcut stock by simmering together 3 qt [2.8 L] of water, shrimp shells, and 6 vegetable bouillon cubes for 30 to 45 minutes.

Creole Tomato Gravy Shrimp

4 TO 6 SERVINGS

Shrimp and grits is a quintessential Southern recipe that has become a brunch staple. I prefer mine at suppertime, but that is neither here nor there. The tomato-laden sauce offers a refreshing pop of acid that balances the richness of the grits, and the pairing with Baked Corn Grits (page 125) elevates and perfects this classic combo.

FOR THE CREOLE TOMATO GRAVY

½ cup [115 g] unsalted butter

½ cup [65 g] all-purpose flour

2 cups [450 g] chopped andouille sausage, sliced ⅓ in [8 mm] thick

1 cup [150 g] chopped onion

1 cup [150 g] chopped celery

1 cup [150 g] chopped bell pepper

2 cups [300 g] chopped fresh okra, sliced into ⅓ in [8 mm] rounds

4 garlic cloves, minced

One 28 oz [790 g] can crushed tomatoes

6 to 8 cups [1.4 to 1.9 L] Shellfish Stock (page 148)

2 bay leaves

2 sprigs fresh thyme

1 Tbsp Old Bay seasoning

Salt

1 Tbsp filé powder (or 4 bay leaves)

FOR THE SHRIMP

2 Tbsp unsalted butter

1 lb [450 g] medium/large shrimp, peeled and deveined

Juice of 1 lemon

¼ tsp Old Bay seasoning

Salt

FOR SERVING

Baked Corn Grits (page 125)

½ cup [10 g] chopped parsley, for garnish

½ cup [50 g] chopped green onion, for garnish

Crystal or Tabasco hot sauce, for garnish

cont'd

To make the tomato gravy: In a large Dutch oven over medium-low heat, melt the butter, then slowly whisk in the flour. Cook the roux for 15 minutes, whisking constantly, until it is dark brown, the color of milk chocolate. Turn down the heat to low, then add the sausage, onions, celery, and bell pepper and cook for 10 more minutes, stirring constantly with a wooden spoon, until it is a deep, dark brown color. Add the okra, garlic, tomatoes and cook for 5 more minutes.

Using a large ladle, gradually add the shellfish stock, letting it incorporate after each addition. Continue adding stock until the gumbo reaches a nappe consistency (see page 37). Add the bay leaves, thyme, and Old Bay seasoning and season with salt. Simmer over low heat for at least 30 minutes or up to 6 hours, and finish with filé powder just before removing from the heat.

To cook the shrimp: In a large skillet over high heat, melt the butter. Pat the shrimp dry and add to the skillet, cooking on just one side for 2 to 3 minutes, or until just pink. Season with a squeeze of lemon, Old Bay, and a dash of salt.

To serve: Scoop the grits into a bowl, top with the shrimp, then pour the gravy over the top. Garnish with the parsley, green onion, and hot sauce.

152

Cornmeal Catfish with Green Goddess Dressing

4 TO 6 SERVINGS

I love to fish, and catfish is so easy and enjoyable to catch. You gotta love a hobby where you sit in a chair, holding an ice-cold beer in one hand and a fishin' pole in the other. There are a million ways to eat the flaky, mild meat of catfish, but my all-time favorite is a fish fry. It's a social gathering where everyone is invited to join in on the prep. This catfish is delicious with Birthday Pickled Salad (page 86) and this cool, refreshing Green Goddess Dressing. Invite some friends over and try this one ASAP!

5 cups [1.2 L] buttermilk

1 cup [240 ml] dill pickle juice

8 to 10 dashes Crystal hot sauce

3 lb [1.2 kg] catfish, cut into 6 oz [170 g] fillets, skin removed, cleaned, and patted dry

Canola oil, for frying (8 to 10 cups [1.9 to 2.4 L])

3 cups [375 g] all-purpose flour

2 cups [260 g] fine ground cornmeal

2 Tbsp garlic powder

1 Tbsp onion powder

1 Tbsp celery salt

1 tsp freshly ground black pepper

1 tsp cayenne pepper

Salt

Green Goddess Dressing (recipe follows)

In a flat dish or pan or in a large ziplock bag, combine the buttermilk, pickle juice, and hot sauce. Brine the catfish in the mixture for at least 1 hour or up to overnight.

Fill a deep pot or fryer halfway with the oil and heat to 350°F [175°C]. Set a cooling rack in a tray or line a plate with paper towels. In a medium bowl, stir together the flour, cornmeal, garlic and onion powders, celery salt, black pepper, and cayenne until combined. Dredge the catfish, following the dredging instructions from Bee's Fried Chicken (see page 181). Repeat until all the fish fillets are dredged.

cont'd

Deep fry the fish for 7 to 8 minutes, or until the fish is golden brown and crispy. Place on the prepared rack or paper towels to absorb excess oil. Sprinkle with salt and enjoy immediately with a side of Green Goddess Dressing for dipping.

Green Goddess Dressing
—— 2 CUPS [480 ML]

1 cup [240 g] mayonnaise

½ cup [75 g] chopped onion

½ cup [75 g] chopped cucumber

½ ripe avocado

¼ cup [5 g] fresh parsley

¼ cup [5 g] fresh dill fronds

¼ cup [5 g] fresh cilantro

1 garlic clove

2 Tbsp fresh lemon juice

1 tsp freshly ground black pepper

¼ tsp celery salt

¼ cup [60 ml] canola or grapeseed oil

Salt

Combine everything except the oil and salt in a food processor. While processing, slowly add the oil until the dressing is smooth. Season with salt. Enjoy immediately or keep refrigerated in an airtight container for up to 4 days.

Salt-Crusted Fish with Aji Verde Sauce

4 TO 6 SERVINGS

This fish recipe is from culinary school and has been serving me well since graduation. It is a simple, showstopper dish, my favorite kind. I love serving this for an intimate party, placing it in the middle of the table for guests to share from. Top it with Aji Verde Sauce and serve with a side of BLT Butter Bean Salad (page 89) for your new go-to dinner party menu.

4 cups [1.2 kg] salt

3 egg whites

Zest and juice of 2 lemons

8 sprigs fresh rosemary

8 sprigs thyme

4 bay leaves

2 Tbsp dried fennel

2 Tbsp whole black peppercorns

3 lb [1.2 kg] whole white fish with skin, tail, and head on, gutted (red snapper, grouper, dorado, sea bass, haddock, and even salmon all work)

2 Tbsp finishing-quality olive oil

Aji Verde Sauce (recipe follows)

Preheat the oven to 400°F [205°C]. Line a large rimmed sheet pan with foil or parchment paper and set aside.

In a large bowl, mix the salt with the egg whites and juice of 1 lemon until it resembles moist sand. Strip the leaves from half of the rosemary and thyme sprigs and stir into the mixture along with 2 of the bay leaves and the fennel, peppercorns, and zest of 1 lemon.

Spread half of the salt mixture in the center of the sheet pan and place the remaining rosemary and thyme sprigs and bay leaves on top. Lay the fish on the mound, then cover with the remaining salt mixture, lightly packing it to completely cover the fish.

cont'd

157

Bake the fish for 30 minutes, or until the salt crust is rock hard on the outside and very light golden. Add 10 minutes of additional cooking time for every 1 lb [450 g] over 3 lb [1.2 kg] your fish is (for example, 40 minutes for 4 lb [1.8 kg]). Remove from the oven and let stand for 10 minutes.

With the dull side of a heavy chef's knife, crack the top of the salt crust and carefully discard it, being sure not to leave a lot of excess salt on the fish. With your hands, peel back the skin from the top of the fish and discard. Using a fish spatula, carefully transfer the top fillet to a platter. Flip the fish over and repeat the process. Drizzle with the olive oil and the remaining lemon juice and zest. Enjoy immediately with the Aji Verde Sauce alongside.

Aji Verde Sauce
—— MAKES 2 CUPS [480 ML]

¾ cup [20 g] packed fresh cilantro leaves with a few stems

¼ cup [60 g] mayonnaise

¼ cup [60 g] queso fresco or blanco

1 Tbsp prepared aji amarillo paste (available in the Hispanic section of the grocery store)

2 medium jalapeños, with seeds, chopped

3 garlic cloves

Juice of 1 lime

½ tsp salt, plus more to taste

¼ cup [60 ml] olive oil

Combine the cilantro, mayonnaise, queso, aji amarillo paste, jalapeños, garlic, lime juice, and salt in a food processor. Process on low speed until combined and chopped, then while processing, drizzle in the olive oil and ¼ cup [60 ml] of water, alternating additions, until combined. Taste and adjust the salt.

➤ NOTE ◄
I am not a huge fan of leftover fish, but it does often happen with this recipe. My favorite next-day use is to sandwich it between tortillas and all the fixins (see Homemade Salsa, page 67, and Bomb Nacho toppings, page 65) for the best fish tacos, even a day later!

gs & lthy

Deviled Eggs

Eggs are my favorite food group. I like them in every form, in every fashion, and have always been enthralled by their shape-shifting ways. They can aerate, leaven, and act as a sauce all on their own. They can be the base of the lowest-calorie dishes or the main component of the richest soufflé.

Today, I have fifteen chickens in my backyard coop—affectionately known as the "chicken chalet"—that I built with one of my employees in the heat of summer (a story for another time). It's painted white to match our house, has a tin roof and black windows, and is outfitted with a fan, heater, and twinkle lights. God forbid the ladies get hot, cold, or spend a night in the dark.

My absolute favorite way to enjoy my absolute favorite food from these ladies is deviled. Deviled eggs are quintessentially Southern and my go-to dish to bring to an event. They can be black tie or beach picnic. I've made them in more ways than I can count, but this classic recipe and its dressed-up variations will always be my best in show.

Classic Deviled Eggs
—— 12 SERVINGS

6 eggs

¼ cup [60 g] mayonnaise

1 tsp stone ground mustard

¼ tsp onion powder

¼ tsp garlic powder

¼ tsp paprika

Salt

Freshly ground black pepper

How to boil the perfect egg: Completely submerge the eggs in a saucepot filled with cold water. Bring to a boil, then immediately turn off the heat and cover. Set a timer for 8 minutes and let stand, covered, until the timer goes off. Immediately pour out the hot water and fill the pot with ice. Let sit for 5 minutes before peeling (see Note, facing page).

How to make the perfect filling: Halve the eggs vertically using a sharp knife. Using a small spoon, carefully scoop out the yolks and place them in a small bowl. Place the egg whites on a plate and set aside. In a food processor, combine the yolks, mayonnaise, mustard, onion powder, garlic powder, and paprika and mix until completely smooth. With the processor switched off, scrape down the sides of the bowl with a rubber spatula to be sure all the ingredients are incorporated and the mixture is smooth. Season with salt and pepper. Use a piping bag with a medium round tip to fill the hollows in the egg whites.

cont'd

Wicked Chickens
—— 12 SERVINGS

¼ cup [57 g] chopped smoked brisket or cooked bacon

2 Tbsp barbecue sauce

12 Fried Pickled Okra (page 57), cut into ½ in [12 mm] rounds

½ cup [75 g] chopped celery leaves

Prepare a dozen Classic Deviled Eggs (facing page). Garnish the prepared deviled eggs with brisket or bacon, drizzle with barbecue sauce, top with okra, and sprinkle with celery leaves.

Crab Crunch Roll
—— 12 SERVINGS

¼ cup [60 g] Grandmama's West Indies Crab Salad (page 142)

¼ cup [60 ml] yum yum sauce (can be found in the Asian food section of most grocery stores)

¼ cup [25 g] tempura crunch (can be found in the Asian food section of most grocery stores or online)

Prepare a dozen Classic Deviled Eggs (facing page). Place about 1 tsp of the crab salad on each egg. Drizzle with yum yum sauce, then sprinkle with tempura crunch to mimic a sushi roll.

✦ NOTE ✦

I love making the Wicked Chickens the day after I serve brisket. It's a great way to reinvent the leftovers! Or use brisket from your local grocery store or restaurant.

⋯⋯ NOTE ⋯⋯

For ease of peeling, you must peel the eggs right after they've been cooked (after the specified 5-minute wait). I cannot emphasize this enough. The longer they sit, the more they commit to keeping that shell on nice and tight. Here's how to do it: Crack the larger, flat bottom part of the egg (referred to as the "air pocket") and peel a small shell piece off with your fingers. Gently roll the egg over a towel to crack the shell all the way around—it should look like shattered glass. Slip a spoon under the shell so that the curve of the spoon follows the curve of the egg. Rotate the egg and move the spoon to peel back the shell. Dip the egg back into cold water to clean off any remaining shell.

167

Green Eggs and Ham
—— 12 SERVINGS

CHIMICHURRI

1 cup [150 g] chopped onion

¾ cup [180 ml] extra-virgin olive oil

½ cup [120 ml] red wine vinegar

½ cup [10 g] chopped cilantro

¼ cup [5 g] chopped flat-leaf parsley

3 or 4 garlic cloves

1 tsp salt, plus more to taste

PICKLED MUSTARD SEEDS

1 cup [170 g] dried mustard seeds

½ cup [120 ml] apple cider vinegar

¼ tsp salt

HERB SALAD

¼ cup [5 g] chopped flat-leaf parsley

2 Tbsp whole dill fronds

2 Tbsp minced chives

2 Tbsp chopped tarragon leaves

½ cup [110 g] thinly sliced
country ham or prosciutto

To make the chimichurri: Combine the onion, oil, vinegar, cilantro, parsley, garlic, and salt in a food processor and purée until smooth. Taste and adjust the salt. Set aside.

To make the pickled mustard seeds: Combine the mustard seeds, vinegar, 2 cups [480 ml] of water, and the salt in a small saucepan over medium heat and bring to a boil. Immediately lower the heat to low and simmer for 20 minutes, or until tender. Strain and let cool before using. If not using immediately, keep refrigerated in an airtight container for up to 3 months.

To make the herb salad: Toss the herbs together in a small bowl. Pro tip: You can do this the day before, cover them with ice water, and refrigerate overnight. Simply drain and dry the herbs on a paper towel when ready to use. They'll be as fresh as if you just picked them.

To assemble: Prepare a dozen Classic Deviled Eggs (page 166). Top each with a slice of ham, a drizzle of chimichurri, a sprinkle of herb salad, and a dollop of mustard seeds.

Baptism Quiche

6 TO 8 SERVINGS

It is my observation that meat-n-three still reigns supreme here in the South. That is, until it is time for a baby's baptism. When it comes to celebrating a baptism, we bring out the adorable, eggy brunch pies and accompany them with frisée salads and fruit. It's as if we are matching the menu with our baby's baptism gown—all delicacy and innocence.

While delicious, these menus are sparse on substance to fill you up. Years ago, as I prepared for my fifty-somethingth catered baptism party, I came up with a solution to please everyone: quiche for those seeking dainty fare and Breakfast Casserole (page 173) for those seeking hearty sustenance.

This is the base recipe I use for the best quiche. I swap out fillings depending on what I have on hand or what my client requests. This is a recipe where, if you're short on time, you can use a store-bought crust without missing too much.

1½ cups [360 ml] whole milk

3 eggs

¼ tsp salt

¼ tsp freshly ground black pepper

⅛ tsp nutmeg

One 9 in [23 cm] pie shell, blind-baked (see Classic Pie Dough, page 231) or store-bought

Preheat the oven to 350°F [175°C]. In a medium bowl, whisk together the milk, eggs, salt, pepper, and nutmeg. Set aside.

Place the filling ingredients (choose from the selections that follow) in the prepared pie shell. Pour the egg mixture over the fillings. Bake for 35 to 45 minutes, or until the middle is set and an inserted knife comes out clean. Let cool for 15 minutes before slicing.

cont'd

Bacon, Spinach, and Mushroom Quiche

—

1½ cups [225 g] sliced portabella mushrooms

1 tsp olive oil

4 cups [80 g] spinach

3 slices cooked bacon, crumbled

¼ cup [20 g] grated Parmesan cheese

2 Tbsp chopped chives

In a medium sauté pan over medium heat, sauté the mushrooms with the olive oil for 2 minutes. Add the spinach and sauté until it wilts slightly. Transfer the spinach and mushrooms to the prepared pie shell and sprinkle with the bacon, Parmesan cheese, and chives. Follow the remaining directions for Baptism Quiche (page 170).

Creole Crab Quiche

—

½ cup [75 g] chopped bell pepper

1 tsp olive oil

1 cup [225 g] fresh jumbo lump crabmeat

½ cup [50 g] grated pepper Jack cheese

½ cup [55 g] grated Parmesan cheese

¼ cup [25 g] chopped green onions

1 tsp Old Bay seasoning

In a medium sauté pan over medium heat, sauté the bell pepper with the olive oil for 3 minutes. Remove from the heat and stir in the crab, pepper Jack and

Parmesan cheeses, green onions, and Old Bay and transfer the mixture to the pie shell. Follow the remaining directions for Baptism Quiche (page 170).

Goat Cheese and Asparagus Quiche

—

1 cup [150 g] chopped asparagus stalks, ends trimmed, cut into ½ in [12 mm] pieces

1 tsp olive oil

½ cup [50 g] crumbled goat cheese

½ cup [50 g] chopped green onion

¼ cup [5 g] chopped flat-leaf parsley

In a medium sauté pan over medium heat, sauté the asparagus with the olive oil for 3 minutes, or until bright green. In a mixing bowl, using your hands, toss together the asparagus, goat cheese, green onions, and parsley. Transfer the mixture to the prepared pie shell. Follow the remaining directions for Baptism Quiche (page 170).

Breakfast Casserole

This recipe was passed down to my mom by a family friend over a decade ago and we've yet to see a Christmas morning without it since. We typically eat it alongside a pile of cheese grits and one (or two) servings of our homemade cinnamon rolls. In my opinion, it is the definition of comfort food and the best thing to whip up in a pinch.

4 eggs

2 cups [480 ml] whole milk

1 tsp dried mustard

1 tsp salt

1 lb [450 g] ground pork breakfast sausage, browned and drained

8 slices white bread, crusts removed, cubed

2 cups [200 g] packed freshly grated sharp Cheddar cheese

In a large mixing bowl, whisk the eggs, then whisk in the milk. Whisk in the dried mustard and salt. Add the sausage, bread, and cheese and stir to incorporate. Let sit at room temperature for 30 to 45 minutes or refrigerate overnight.

Preheat the oven to 350°F [175°C]. Butter a 9 by 13 in [23 by 33 cm] casserole dish and pour the mixture into the dish. Cover the dish with foil and bake for 45 minutes, then uncover and bake for 15 more minutes. Let stand for 15 minutes before serving, and enjoy it while still warm.

Supper Club
Smoked Wings with
White Barbecue Sauce

3 TO 5 SERVINGS

These "smoked" wings are a great party trick. They get their flavor from smoked paprika and a high cooking temp, which means they are a go-to easy, quick meal when we decide to have friends over at the last minute for what we jokingly refer to as Supper Club. The wings taste as if they've just been pulled off the grill, but they cook in the oven in 15 minutes flat. So invite a few friends, serve these with a side of Alabama White Barbecue Sauce, and see how easy an impromptu dinner party can be!

"SMOKED" WINGS

½ cup [85 g] light brown sugar

¼ cup [60 g] salt

¼ cup [25 g] smoked paprika

1 Tbsp onion powder

1 Tbsp garlic powder

½ tsp ground ginger

5 lb [2.3 kg] chicken wings, rinsed and patted dry

ALABAMA WHITE BARBECUE SAUCE

1 cup [240 g] mayonnaise

¼ cup [60 ml] apple cider vinegar

1 tsp honey

½ tsp Crystal hot sauce

½ tsp smoked paprika

½ tsp salt

½ tsp garlic powder

½ tsp onion powder

½ tsp freshly ground black pepper

Pinch of cayenne pepper

Preheat the oven to 425°F [220°C]. Line a half sheet pan with parchment paper.

To make the wings: In a medium bowl, stir together all the dry ingredients. Add the wings and toss with the dry rub to coat, patting so the rub sticks. Place the wings on the prepared pan and cook for 12 to 15 minutes, or until golden brown and cooked throughout. Let cool for 10 minutes before serving.

To make the sauce: In a medium mixing bowl, whisk together all the ingredients. Enjoy immediately or keep refrigerated in an airtight container for up to 3 months.

Cast Iron Barbecue Chicken Legs

4 TO 8 SERVINGS

I make this recipe at least once a week for my family. This braised chicken is deceptively simple and ridiculously delicious, with a kick. We love it over rice, with a salad, piled on tacos—whatever you do, just prepare to devour!

2 Tbsp salt, plus more to taste

1 Tbsp Tajín Clásico seasoning

8 bone-in, skin-on chicken legs, rinsed and patted dry

¼ cup [60 ml] olive oil

½ cup [120 ml] apple cider vinegar

3 cups [720 ml] chicken stock or broth

½ cup [120 ml] chipotle pepper sauce

¼ cup [60 ml] barbecue sauce (my favorite is Sweet Baby Ray's)

¼ cup [60 ml] Cholula hot sauce

Heat a medium cast iron skillet over low heat. While the skillet is heating, prepare the chicken.

In a small bowl, combine the salt and Tajín seasoning and evenly rub it over the dry chicken legs. Increase the heat to medium-high and add the olive oil. Sear the chicken, fattiest-side down, until golden brown, about 5 minutes. Deglaze the skillet with the vinegar, lower the heat to medium-low, and cook until the vinegar is almost completely reduced, 3 to 5 minutes. Add the chicken stock, chipotle sauce, barbecue sauce, and hot sauce and bring to a simmer over medium heat. Cover and continue to simmer, frequently turning the chicken to thoroughly coat it in sauce, for 45 minutes, or until the chicken is completely cooked and the sauce reaches a nappe consistency (see page 37). Taste and adjust the salt and enjoy immediately. The chicken will keep refrigerated in an airtight container for up to 3 days.

Roasted Chicken and Drippin' Veggies

4 SERVINGS

Mastering a roasted chicken is like mastering the art of conversation. Done poorly, it is dry, bland, and all-around disappointing. Done well, however, it can prompt your love to propose, leave your mother-in-law begging for advice, and make you appear to be a polished hostess. It's deceptively simple and shockingly delicious. It's the gift that keeps on giving—supplying subsequent meals and leftover dishes that are better the next day. It's humble yet decadent and typically elicits a "cannot wait 'til it's cool enough to eat it" type of response. It's a one-pan meal so layered in flavor that your family won't know how you did it. If you're like me, you won't tell them.

★ NOTE ★

I typically double this recipe, making two chickens. We eat the leftovers in salad, stuff it in roasted sweet potatoes, or make tacos. It ends up being our dinner for three days!

ROASTED CHICKEN

1 whole chicken (3 to 5 lb [1.4 to 2.3 kg])

½ cup [120 ml] olive oil

1 Tbsp salt

1 lemon, halved

2 sprigs fresh rosemary

3 Tbsp dried lavender *or* 2 sprigs fresh thyme

1 head garlic, each clove peeled and smashed with the flat side of a knife

DRIPPIN' VEGGIES

3 ears fresh sweet corn, kernels removed

3 cups [70 g] chopped green cabbage

2 cups [300 g] whole cherry or grape tomatoes

1 onion, chopped

2 cups [300 g] black-eyed or lady peas, frozen or fresh

2 cups [450 g] sliced smoked sausage (my favorite is Conecuh)

1 Tbsp salt

To make the roasted chicken: Set a cooling rack on a sheet pan. Pat down the chicken with paper towels and place it on the rack. Refrigerate the chicken, uncovered, overnight or up to 2 days. If you're in a time crunch, instead of refrigerating, whip out your hairdryer and blow it on the chicken skin on the high setting for about 5 minutes. This dries out the skin, which makes the meat hold moisture and the skin crisp like a potato chip.

cont'd

178

Preheat the oven to 425°F [220°C]. Rub the bird down with the oil and sprinkle evenly with the salt. Squeeze the lemon over the chicken, then push the halves into the cavity along with the herbs and garlic.

To truss the chicken, tuck the wings behind the bird's back. Bring the legs together at the ankle as if the chicken is crossing its legs. Wrap a piece of twine around the crossed ankles. Bring the twine over the legs and pull it tight around the back of the chicken. Tie the twine in a bow at the top of the chicken's breast.

To make the veggies: Place the vegetables, peas, and sausage in the bottom of a deep roasting pan. Sprinkle with the salt.

Place the chicken on a cooling rack on top of the veggies. Roast for 1 hour on the middle rack of the oven. Turn the oven off and leave the chicken in the oven for 20 minutes. Remove the chicken and let it stand at room temperature for another 20 minutes. Carve and enjoy the best roasted chicken you've ever had.

180

Bee's Fried Chicken

4 SERVINGS

My mom never really made fried chicken. When we did get it, it usually came in a box shaped like a house and was always slightly cold by the time we ate it. When I first opened my second restaurant, KBC on Foster, I wanted fried chicken on the menu. I became obsessed with mastering the art of the decadent, sinful bird. As you'll see, I am a big believer in dark meat only for fried chicken, y'all! I spent weeks testing recipes with Bee—lovingly known as Queen Bee—the first employee I ever hired. The result of our efforts is Bee's Fried Chicken, which has been served to thousands of customers and brides. It's our most requested item at brunch, lunch, and weddings alike, and I can confidently agree with customers who say, "This is the best damn fried chicken I've ever eaten."

➤ NOTE ◄

To keep your hands from becoming a science fair project, use one hand for touching the brined chicken and the other for dredging. This ensures that only one hand is caked with the glue-like result of brining liquid and flour, giving you more control and lessening your chances of burning your hand in the fryer.

4 cups [960 ml] buttermilk

1 cup [240 ml] dill pickle juice

6 to 8 dashes hot sauce (I like Crystal or Tabasco)

3 lb [1.2 kg] bone-in, skin-on, chicken thighs, legs, or a combo of both, rinsed and patted dry

Canola oil, for frying (at least 8 cups [1.9 L])

6 cups [750 g] all-purpose flour

2 Tbsp salt

1 Tbsp garlic powder

1 Tbsp onion powder

1 tsp freshly ground black pepper

1 tsp cayenne pepper

In a medium mixing bowl, combine the buttermilk, pickle juice, and hot sauce and stir to combine. Add the chicken, turning to completely coat. Cover the bowl with plastic wrap and refrigerate for at least 1 hour or up to 3 days.

Fill a cast iron skillet half full with canola oil and begin warming it on the very lowest heat setting. In a medium mixing bowl, stir together the flour, 1 Tbsp of the salt, the garlic powder, onion powder, black pepper, and cayenne. Dredge the chicken by letting liquid drip off each chicken piece, then coating it in the flour mixture. Pat the flour mixture onto the skin, making sure to turn the chicken and press the flour mixture onto all sides to be sure it is evenly coated. Place the chicken on a plate and set aside.

cont'd

I reuse my flour dredge, buttermilk brine, and oil multiple times before I throw them out. If you do this, be sure you completely clean and dry your chicken before brining. Store the brine and dredge in separate airtight bags in the freezer and defrost when ready to use. For the oil, let cool for at least 1 hour after frying, then strain and place in an airtight container in your pantry for up to 2 months.

Increase the heat to high and heat the oil to 350°F [175°C]. Set a cooling rack inside a half sheet pan. To test whether the oil is hot enough, drop a sprinkle of flour in the pan. If the flour pops and fizzes, the oil is ready.

Place up to 4 pieces of chicken in the oil. Once the chicken is in the oil, immediately turn down the heat to medium to maintain a steady temperature of 300°F to 325°F [150°C to 165°C]. This allows the chicken to cook slowly and evenly throughout while it develops a crispy golden crust. Using a long-handled fork, such as a carving fork, gently flip the chicken over every 2 minutes. Cook for 15 to 18 minutes for breasts, 12 to 15 minutes for thighs, 7 to 10 minutes for legs, or until the chicken reaches an internal temperature of 165°F [74°C]. When the chicken is done, place it on the prepared rack and immediately dust with the remaining 1 Tbsp of salt. Cooling the chicken on a rack allows the excess oil to drip off while leaving the bottom of the chicken crispy. Let cool for 5 minutes, then enjoy immediately or place in the oven preheated to 250°F [120°C] to keep warm until ready to eat.

Bama's Chicken Pot Pie

After a few months of dating my now-husband, I decided it was time to let him meet my close-knit group of childhood friends. Their opinions were important. We met at the local oyster bar for dozens on the half shell, cold beer, and chili dogs. After the first few pints, we all loosened up, and I asked my favorite question: If you were on death row, what would be your last meal?

We took turns sharing our deepest cravings, and then came Deavours's turn. Over the course of our blossoming courtship, I'd made countless chef-worthy meals ranging from champagne and sushi to homemade ravioli and chocolate soufflés. I was no fool that the way to a man's heart is through his stomach, and by God was I gonna keep his full with the finest feasts he'd ever had. Whispers and smirks were passed around the table. How could he possibly choose? Would it be the crawfish boil Kelsey did last week? Or maybe the salt-crusted snapper she caught and cooked that night? He took a sip of his beer and proudly announced that his mom's store-bought crust, chicken pot pie was his all-time favorite meal.

Crickets. Signals for more drinks. Checks, please!

Miraculously, I still married this guy. Today it's a favorite family joke, and one of our chickens goes by the name Pot Pie. I even made a fancied-up version of this dish in honor of Deavours during a memory challenge on *Top Chef*. This recipe is passed down from my mother-in-law—affectionately knows as "Bama"—by way of her mother. My favorite part of her recipe is the unusual addition of boiled eggs. The eggs add a decadent, buttery layer and a velvety texture. It is wholesome, comforting, and, well, easy as pie.

FOR THE FILLING

2 whole Roasted Chickens (page 178) or store-bought rotisserie chickens in a pinch

1 cup [90 g] diced carrots

One 10¾ oz [325 ml] can cream of mushroom soup

2 cups [480 ml] low-sodium chicken broth

1 tsp salt

½ tsp freshly ground black pepper

¼ tsp white pepper

¼ tsp nutmeg

4 eggs, boiled and diced

1 cup [145 g] frozen peas

1 bunch fresh parsley, chopped

FOR THE CRUST

3 cups [375 g] all-purpose flour, plus more for dusting

1½ tsp salt

1 tsp baking powder

¼ tsp sugar

½ cup [115 g] unsalted butter, cold, diced, plus more for greasing the dish

½ cup [120 ml] ice water

1 egg, beaten, for egg wash

Coarse salt

cont'd

To make the filling: Pull off all the chicken meat and place it in a bowl. Set aside.

Blanch the carrots by submerging them in boiling water for 2 minutes, then immediately plunging them into ice water. In a large bowl, whisk together the mushroom soup, chicken broth, salt, black pepper, white pepper, and nutmeg. Add the chicken, eggs, carrots, peas, and parsley. Mix together to coat. Set the bowl aside while you take care of the dough.

To make the crust: Dust a work surface with flour. In a food processor, mix together the flour, salt, baking powder, and sugar. Add the cold butter and pulse until the butter is the size of frozen peas. Continuing to pulse, add the ice water and process only until the dough just comes together. Turn the dough out onto the floured surface and knead quickly into a ball. Wrap the dough in plastic and refrigerate for 30 minutes.

Remove the dough from the fridge and roll it out on the floured surface to an 11 by 15 in [28 by 38 cm] rectangle, about ¼ in [6 mm] thick, so that it's about 2 in [5 cm] larger than the casserole dish you're using, giving space for the dough to overlay.

To assemble: Preheat the oven to 350°F [175°C]. Butter a 9 by 13 in [23 by 33 cm] casserole dish. Pour the filling into the buttered dish, then carefully lay the dough over the filling, allowing it to fold over the sides of the dish. Using kitchen shears, trim the dough around the sides, making it as uniform as possible to promote even baking. Gently press the dough against the sides of the dish to make it stick. Brush the dough with the egg wash and use the tip of a sharp knife to make three slits in the center. Sprinkle with coarse salt. Place the casserole dish on a sheet pan and bake for 30 minutes or until the crust is golden and the filling is hot and bubbling. Let cool slightly before serving.

Seared Duck Breast with Caramelized Orange Butter

2 SERVINGS

In the Deep South, there isn't just one hunting season—there's deer season, quail season, duck season, and turkey season. Just when you're ready for one to be over, the next one starts up. Most avid hunters are eager to have someone else prepare their loot, and I'm always happy to oblige, but you have to clean your game yourself before you show up!

This duck dish is easy to accomplish but could pass for fine dining when plated. The duck is velvety, with the flavor of brown butter and pops of sweet and sour orange blanketing the top. I often serve it accompanied by a simple arugula salad from the garden and Sorghum and Pecan Sweet Potatoes (page 120).

Salt

2 duck breasts, scored with four cuts ¼ in [6 mm] deep at an angle, patted dry

½ cup [115 g] unsalted butter

¼ cup [35 g] chopped onion

¼ cup [80 g] orange segments

¼ cup [60 ml] orange juice

1 sprig thyme

Preheat the oven to 400°F [205°C]. Line a sheet pan with parchment paper. Evenly sprinkle salt on both sides of the duck and set aside.

In a cold, dry cast iron skillet, place the duck skin-side down. Turn the heat to medium-low and let the fat render for exactly 20 minutes. Flip and cook the other side of the duck for 5 minutes. Place the duck, skin-side up, on the prepared pan and roast in the oven for 6 to 8 minutes or until the duck is firm to the touch with a slight give. Duck should not feel completely firm but more like a wet sponge.

In the skillet where the duck was seared, melt the butter over medium-high heat, then add the onions and cook, stirring frequently, until translucent, 3 to 5 minutes. Add the orange segments, orange juice, sprig of thyme, and ¼ tsp of salt, then immediately turn down the heat to low. Simmer, stirring frequently, allowing the liquid to reduce to a sauce, for 12 to 15 minutes, or until it has reached a nappe consistency (see page 37). Set aside.

Remove the duck from the oven, let it rest for 10 minutes, and slice each breast at a 45-degree angle into ¼ in [6 mm] thick strips. Properly cooked duck should resemble medium-rare steak. If the duck is still very rare, pop it back in the oven for 1 to 2 more minutes. Arrange the slices in a fanlike pattern and spoon the orange butter sauce over the top. Serve immediately.

Euro
Beef

Church Barnard's Spaghetti Sauce

When I was growing up, my dad rarely cooked. Sure, he grilled outside, but I have very few memories of him in the kitchen. The exception was spaghetti sauce day. His dad, Church, was known for his spaghetti sauce, and my dad would make a giant pot of his recipe two or three times a year. We'd all help in the process of chopping, stirring, bagging, and freezing. We'd be stocked like the apocalypse was coming and would joke that if you ever visited our house and the freezer was devoid of spaghetti sauce, something was really wrong. I still make it in giant batches today and swear up and down that it's better when it's been reheated from frozen.

½ cup [120 ml] olive oil

4 large onions, chopped

1 green bell pepper, chopped

2 Tbsp salt, plus more to taste

8 garlic cloves, minced

8 oz [225 g] white mushrooms, sliced

3 lb [1.2 kg] ground beef

Two 6 oz [177 g] cans tomato paste

Two 28 oz [1.5 kg] cans crushed tomatoes

One 5¾ oz [170 ml] jar Spanish olives, sliced

One 3½ oz [110 ml] jar capers, drained

3 bay leaves

1 tsp dried thyme

1 tsp dried oregano

1 tsp marjoram

½ tsp dried tarragon

½ tsp cumin

½ tsp mace

In a large pot over medium-low heat, heat the oil, then add the onions, bell pepper, and salt. Let cook, stirring frequently, for 10 to 12 minutes, or until translucent. Add the garlic and cook, stirring frequently, for 2 more minutes. Add the mushrooms and beef and continue to cook, stirring frequently, for 15 to 20 minutes, or until the meat has lightly browned. Add the tomato paste and continue to cook for 10 minutes, stirring to coat the meat. Add all the remaining ingredients and bring to a simmer. Cook over low heat, simmering, for a minimum of 2 hours or up to 10 hours. Season with salt and enjoy immediately over pasta, or freeze the sauce in airtight containers for up to 6 months.

Venison Chili

4 TO 6 SERVINGS

Come deer season, I am often gifted with venison from avid hunters happy to share their bounty. I started subbing ground venison for my traditional ground beef and love the way its rich, earthy taste adds depth to this classic fall dish. I make huge batches when I can and freeze them. Off the record, they still taste delicious after even a year in the freezer.

◾ NOTE ◾

If not enjoying immediately, refrigerate in airtight containers for up to 3 days or freeze for up to 6 months.

1 Tbsp olive oil

2 lb [900 g] ground venison

2 large onions, chopped

1 bell pepper, chopped

3 stalks celery, chopped

2 garlic cloves, chopped

1 Tbsp salt, plus more to taste

1 cup [240 ml] lager beer

2 Tbsp chili powder

1 tsp ground cumin

¼ tsp cayenne pepper

One 28 oz can [790 ml] diced tomatoes

One 15 oz [430 g] can kidney beans, drained and rinsed

One 15 oz [440 ml] can pinto beans, drained and rinsed

One 8 oz [240 ml] can tomato sauce

2 bay leaves

One 16 oz bag [450 g] tortilla chips, for garnish

1 lime, cut into wedges, for garnish

2 cups [200 g] freshly shredded Cheddar cheese, for garnish

1 cup [100 g] chopped green onions, for garnish

1 cup [240 g] sour cream, for garnish

Crystal hot sauce, for garnish (optional)

In a large pot over medium-low heat, heat the oil, then add the venison. Cook until lightly browned, about 5 minutes, stirring and breaking up clumps. Add the onions, bell pepper, celery, garlic, and salt and cook, stirring frequently, until slightly translucent, about 5 minutes. Add the beer, then cook until the liquid has completely reduced, 5 to 8 minutes. Add the chili powder, cumin, and cayenne and stir to coat. Add the diced tomatoes, kidney and pinto beans, tomato sauce, and bay leaves. Bring to a boil, then lower the heat to low and simmer for at least 30 minutes or up to 4 hours, stirring occasionally. Season with salt. Ladle into bowls; serve with tortilla chips, lime wedges, Cheddar cheese, green onions, sour cream, and hot sauce, if using.

Girl Boss Steak with Confit Onions and Mushrooms

1 SERVING

There is a pecking order to any restaurant kitchen staff. In fine dining, working your way up through the ranks of the kitchen begins with garde manger, and the last step before sous chef is always meat. Earning your spot as meat entremetier means you've almost made it, one step closer to the head of the kitchens. As a young cook starting out, I looked up to that position the most and did everything I could to soak up the knowledge it takes to get there. When a woman was on meat in a kitchen, I considered her an absolute girl boss. Not only did she have the talent to work her way up, but also the grit and dedication to survive the trenches of a mostly male-dominated industry. This steak is an ode to all the girl bosses out there—a classic, badass, restaurant-style steak, basted in butter, cooked over spitting heat to utter perfection, and finished with a pan sauce.

1 steak of choice, at least 2 in [5 cm] thick (I prefer a thick-cut, 10 oz [280 g] bone-in ribeye)

½ cup [115 g] unsalted butter

1 cup [150 g] mushrooms, halved (oyster, portabella, hen of the woods, or cremini are ideal but choose whatever type looks freshest)

1 onion, sliced

½ cup [120 ml] balsamic vinegar

1 Tbsp soy sauce

1 Tbsp Worcestershire sauce

1 tsp salt

½ cup [115 g] unsalted butter, at room temperature

1 head garlic, about ½ in [12 mm] cut off the top

2 sprigs thyme

1 sprig rosemary

To thoroughly dry the steak, pat it with paper towels and let it sit at room temperature for 1 to 2 hours prior to cooking. (Drying the steak ahead of time produces the best sear.)

In a small skillet over high heat, melt 4 Tbsp [58 g] of the butter. Add the mushrooms and sear until they are golden brown, 2 to 3 minutes. Remove the mushrooms and set aside. Add the onions and sear for 3 minutes, stirring. Add the mushrooms back, along with the remaining 4 Tbsp [58 g] of butter, the balsamic vinegar, soy sauce, and Worcestershire, then immediately lower the heat to low. Simmer for roughly 15 minutes, allowing the liquid to reduce to a sauce.

cont'd

When ready to cook the steak, preheat the oven to 400°F [205°C]. Season each side of the steak with ½ tsp of the salt and set aside. Heat a large cast iron skillet over very high heat until it is almost smoking. Test the heat by putting a small amount of butter in the skillet. If the butter pops and immediately melts, the skillet is ready. Add 2 Tbsp of the butter and as soon as it melts completely, add the steak. Once the steak hits the skillet, do not move it. Let the steak sear over high heat until the bottom side is completely golden brown and cooked evenly, 2 to 3 minutes. Carefully tilt the skillet, firmly holding the steak in place with a spoon or spatula, and drain out the butter. Add another 2 Tbsp of the butter, then flip the steak and sear for 1 minute on the other side.

Add the remaining 4 Tbsp [58 g] of butter and the garlic (cut-side down), thyme, and rosemary to the skillet, then baste the steak by tilting the skillet to one side and using a spoon to gently pour the butter over the top of the steak. Baste 6 to 8 times before finishing the steak.

To finish the steak to the desired doneness, choose from the following directions (note that these times are based on a 2 in [5 cm], 10 oz [280 g] bone-in ribeye, and may need to be adjusted according to the thickness and cut of meat):

Rare: Remove the steak from the skillet.

Medium rare: Transfer the skillet to the oven for 2 minutes.

Medium: Transfer the skillet to the oven for 4 minutes.

Medium well: Transfer the skillet to the oven for 6 to 8 minutes.

Well done: Transfer the skillet to the oven for 10 to 12 minutes.

Transfer the steak to a cutting board to rest for 10 to 15 minutes. Then spoon confit mushrooms with sauce over the steak, being sure to get all the bits out of the pan. Serve and enjoy immediately.

Rosemary and Garlic Pork Tenderloin

4 TO 6 SERVINGS

My mom was a routine-oriented cook, with certain days designated for specific dishes. This pork tenderloin was in the weekly rotation; even so, I never tired of it. I make this version for my family a few times a month, often pairing it with roasted sweet potatoes or cauliflower and a simple arugula salad. It's clean, light, and affordable and is a family favorite all over again.

✦ NOTE ✦

I always have a jar of Chimichurri (page 169) in the fridge, and we love it with this dish. Simply brush a thin layer over the top of the meat while it's resting to add another delicious layer of flavor.

1 Tbsp salt

1 tsp garlic powder

1 tsp onion powder

1 tsp ground coriander

1 tsp dried thyme

1¼ lb [560 g] pork tenderloin

¼ cup [60 ml] olive oil

3 Tbsp unsalted butter

2 garlic cloves, minced

2 sprigs rosemary

Salt

Preheat the oven to 450°F [230°C]. In a small bowl, mix together the salt, garlic powder, onion powder, coriander, and thyme. Stir the mixture with a fork until all the ingredients are well combined. Sprinkle the rub over the tenderloin with a dry hand, turning and pressing the tenderloin gently so the seasoning adheres well to the meat.

In a large skillet over high heat, add the olive oil. Add the tenderloin to the pan and cook, using tongs to turn the meat and searing each side until golden brown, for about 10 minutes total.

Place the butter, garlic, and rosemary in the skillet. Place the skillet in the oven, uncovered, and roast for 10 minutes. Remove from the oven and let cool at room temperature for at least 10 minutes. Slice ½ in [12 mm] thick and serve, or refrigerate in an airtight container with the cooking juices for up to 3 days.

Skillet Baby Back Ribs with Szechuan Barbecue Sauce

4 TO 6 SERVINGS

These fall-off-the-bone, no-grill-needed ribs are to die for and will give your "grill 'em all day ribs" a run for their money. The Szechuan Barbecue Sauce completely sends them over the edge. The Szechuan peppers are a unique and unexpected surprise with every bite of this tender pork.

½ cup [85 g] light brown sugar

¼ cup [60 g] salt

¼ cup [25 g] smoked paprika

1 Tbsp onion powder

1 Tbsp garlic powder

½ tsp ground ginger

3 lb [1.2 kg] pork loin back ribs, trimmed and completely dry

2 Tbsp olive oil

Szechuan Barbecue Sauce (recipe follows)

Preheat the oven to 300°F [150°C]. Line a sheet pan with foil. While you prepare the meat, begin to heat a skillet over low, low heat. This heats the skillet evenly, which allows for better searing.

In a small mixing bowl, stir together the brown sugar, salt, paprika, onion powder, garlic powder, and ginger. Rub the mixture evenly over both sides of the ribs, pressing to ensure it is fully coated and sticking to the meat.

Increase the heat to high and add the oil. Add one slab of ribs, fat-side down, and cook, using tongs to turn the meat and searing each side until golden brown, for about 10 minutes total. Place the seared ribs on the prepared pan, then repeat the searing with the other slab of ribs. Once both slabs are seared, cover with foil and roast for 2 hours.

cont'd

After 2 hours, remove from the oven, uncover, and brush evenly with about one-third to half of the barbecue sauce. Increase the oven temperature to 350°F [175°C] and cook, uncovered, for 30 more minutes. Remove the ribs from the oven and let rest for 20 minutes. While resting, strain the liquid from the pan and whisk it into the remaining barbecue sauce. Slice and serve the ribs immediately with the barbecue sauce on the side or store in airtight containers in the refrigerator for up to 3 days.

◾ NOTE ◾

Any time I am planning to sear meat, I remove it from the package, pat it down to dry it thoroughly, then let it sit out on the counter on paper towels, uncovered, for at least 2 hours. This ensures that the meat properly dries out and also allows it to reach room temperature. This simple step will help you achieve a perfect sear.

Szechuan Barbecue Sauce
—— 2½ CUPS [600 ML]

2 dried Szechuan peppers

2 cups [520 g] ketchup

½ cup [120 ml] apple cider vinegar

2 Tbsp chipotle peppers, puréed

2 Tbsp light brown sugar

1 Tbsp yellow mustard

1 Tbsp Worcestershire sauce

¼ tsp freshly ground black pepper

In a medium saucepan over medium-high heat, toast the peppers for 2 to 3 minutes. Add the ketchup, vinegar, puréed chipotle peppers, sugar, mustard, Worcestershire sauce, and pepper and whisk together to completely incorporate. Bring to a boil, then lower the heat and simmer for 30 minutes to 1 hour. Enjoy immediately or keep refrigerated in an airtight container for up to 6 months.

Cuban Braised Pork Butt

A cook who worked for me for years was originally from Miami; his parents were Cuban. He made me his pulled pork one day to try on our Cuban sandwich, and the rest is history. It's tangy, with a hint of heat, and incredibly versatile. My favorite ways to enjoy it are piled on nachos, in tacos, or served over beans and rice.

★ NOTE ★

To store, portion into airtight containers with the cooking juices and refrigerate for up to 3 days or freeze for up to 6 months.

2 Tbsp garlic powder

2 Tbsp onion powder

2 Tbsp salt

4 lb [1.8 kg] boneless pork shoulder, patted completely dry

3 Tbsp olive oil

2 cups [480 ml] orange juice

2 cups [480 ml] hot sauce (I like Frank's RedHot)

2 cups [480 ml] mojo marinade sauce (I like Badia brand)

1 medium onion, chopped

6 garlic cloves, chopped

2 bay leaves

Salt

Freshly ground black pepper

Preheat the oven to 325°F [165°C]. In a small bowl, mix together the garlic and onion powders and salt until well combined. Sprinkle over the pork with a dry hand, and turn and press the rub into the pork so it adheres.

In a large Dutch oven over high heat, heat the olive oil. Add the pork to the pan and sear for 3 minutes on each side, or until golden brown. Add the orange juice, hot sauce, mojo marinade, onion, garlic, and bay leaves and bring to a simmer. Cover the Dutch oven, then transfer to the oven and braise, basting with liquid every hour, until the pork shoulder is tender and falling apart, 4 to 6 hours.

Once cooked, remove the pork from the braising liquid and let rest for 20 minutes. Shred the pork into bite-size pieces, then set aside. Skim the fat from the braising liquid in the Dutch oven, then reduce the liquid over medium-high heat to about 1½ cups [360 ml]. Season with salt and pepper. Return the pork to the liquid and toss to combine. Serve immediately.

Pot Roast and Leftover French Dip Sandwiches

My brother was—and still is—a notorious anti-dessert person. He most frequently and comically would opt for an additional portion of protein in lieu of the traditional last course of dessert. This pot roast has always been his very favorite meal, and every time I make it I think of his extra "dessert bowl" of pot roast. We now have this on our menu at KBC, and, in case you're wondering, it's my brother's order every single time.

Pot Roast
—— 8 TO 12 SERVINGS

2 Tbsp garlic powder

2 Tbsp onion powder

2 Tbsp salt

4 lb [1.8 kg] beef chuck, patted completely dry

3 Tbsp olive oil

4 cups [960 ml] beef broth

1 cup [240 ml] Worcestershire sauce

1 cup [240 ml] soy sauce

1 medium onion, chopped

6 garlic cloves, chopped

2 bay leaves

Preheat the oven to 325°F [165°C]. In a small bowl, mix together the garlic powder, onion powder, and salt. Stir the mixture with a fork until all the ingredients are well combined. Sprinkle the seasoning over the chuck with a dry hand, then rub the chuck with the seasoning over both sides, pressing gently so the seasoning adheres well.

In a large Dutch oven over high heat, heat the olive oil. Add the chuck to the pan and sear for about 3 minutes on each side until brown, using tongs to turn the meat. Once seared, add the broth, Worcestershire, soy sauce, onion, garlic, and bay leaves and bring to a simmer. Cover with a lid and braise in the oven, basting with liquid every hour, until the chuck is very tender and falling apart, 3 to 4 hours.

cont'd

Once cooked, remove the chuck from the braising liquid and let rest for 20 minutes. Cut the meat into bite-size pieces, then set aside. Skim the fat from the braising liquid in the Dutch oven, then simmer over medium-high heat until it reduces to about 2 cups [480 ml]. Set aside this jus for dipping the sandwiches. Serve immediately or portion with the jus in airtight containers and refrigerate for up to 3 days or freeze for up to 6 months.

Leftover French Dip Sandwiches
—— 4 SANDWICHES

4 Tbsp [58 g] unsalted butter

2 small onions, sliced

4 hoagie rolls

2 cups [260 g] Pot Roast (page 203)

8 slices swiss cheese

Preheat the oven to 350°F [175°C]. In a medium skillet over medium heat, melt 2 Tbsp of the butter, then add the onions and cook until caramelized, 5 to 8 minutes. Remove from the heat and set aside.

Brush the remaining butter over the tops of the hoagie rolls and toast in the oven, whole, for 3 to 6 minutes, or until golden brown. Remove from the oven, then split the hoagies in half lengthwise so they are open-faced. Place roughly ½ cup [65 g] of the meat in each hoagie, top with 2 slices of cheese, then evenly divide the caramelized onions to top each sandwich. Return to the oven, open-faced, and bake for 5 to 8 minutes, or until the cheese is melted and golden. Fold the top half of each hoagie and cut the sandwiches diagonally in half. Serve with the reserved pot roast jus in ramekins or small bowls for dipping. Enjoy immediately.

KBC Country Fried Steak

4 TO 6 SERVINGS

We put this on the menu at KBC one winter and it was an instant classic. Served with Smashed Crispy Potatoes (page 118), it has all the traditional Southern nods—fried, gravy, rich starch—but it is sprinkled with fresh herbs and finished with an arugula salad tossed with slivered grapes and champagne vinaigrette. These additions brighten this deliciously rich meal. It reflects the way I cook Southern food—respecting and perfecting the classics, elevating flavors with a personal twist, and adding something green—and it's become one of my signature dishes.

FOR THE COUNTRY FRIED STEAK

4 cups [960 ml] buttermilk

1 cup [240 ml] dill pickle juice

1 egg

6 to 8 dashes Crystal hot sauce

3 lb [1.2 kg] cube steak (round steak that's been extra tenderized)

6 cups [750 g] all-purpose flour

1 Tbsp garlic powder

1 Tbsp onion powder

1 Tbsp salt

1 tsp freshly ground black pepper

1 tsp cayenne pepper

½ cup [120 ml] canola or vegetable oil

FOR THE BLACK PEPPER GRAVY

⅓ cup [45 g] all-purpose flour

3 to 4 cups [720 to 960 ml] whole milk

½ tsp celery salt

Freshly ground black pepper

1 Tbsp chopped tarragon

1 Tbsp chopped parsley

FOR THE ARUGULA AND GRAPE SALAD

2 Tbsp champagne vinegar

¼ tsp honey

¼ cup [60 ml] olive oil

4 cups [80 g] arugula

½ cup [60 g] slivered green grapes

¼ tsp salt

Smashed Crispy Potatoes (page 118)

To make the steak: Begin by brining the meat. In a medium mixing bowl, combine the buttermilk, pickle juice, egg, and hot sauce and stir to combine. Add the meat, turning to completely coat. Cover with plastic wrap and refrigerate for at least 1 hour or up to 3 days.

cont'd

In a medium mixing bowl, stir together the flour, garlic powder, onion powder, salt, black pepper, and cayenne. Dredge the meat by letting the liquid drip off the beef pieces, then coating in the flour mixture. Pat the flour mixture into the beef, turning and pressing to be sure the meat is evenly coated. Place the beef on a plate and set aside.

In a large cast iron skillet over medium-high heat, heat the oil to 350°F [175°C]. To test whether the oil is hot enough, drop a sprinkle of flour into the pan. If the flour pops and fizzes, the oil is ready. Cook the meat, three pieces at a time, using tongs to turn the pieces over, until the edges start to look golden brown, about 2 minutes on each side. Transfer the meat to a cooling rack set inside a sheet pan or a paper towel–lined plate. Repeat until all the meat is cooked.

To keep the cooked pieces warm while frying the rest, place an oven-safe plate or tray in the oven preheated to 300°F [150°C]. After all the meat is fried, pour the fat into a heatproof bowl. Without cleaning the skillet, return it to the stove over medium-low heat. Add ¼ cup [60 ml] of the fat back to the skillet and allow it to heat up.

To make the gravy: When the fat is hot, sprinkle the flour evenly over the fat. Whisk the two to create a blonde roux. Add more flour if the roux looks overly fatty; add a little more fat if it becomes too clumpy. Whisk and cook until the roux is a deep golden brown. Pour in 3 cups of milk, whisking constantly. Add the celery salt, season with black pepper, and cook, whisking, until the gravy is smooth and thick, 5 to 10 minutes. If it becomes too thick, be prepared to add more milk. Taste and adjust the seasoning. Remove the gravy from the heat and stir in the tarragon and parsley.

To make the salad: In a medium mixing bowl, whisk together the vinegar and honey, then while whisking, slowly drizzle in the olive oil until combined. Add the arugula, grapes, and salt, then toss until evenly coated with the dressing. Set aside.

To assemble: Place the KBC Country Fried Steak over a scoop of Smashed Crispy Potatoes, then add a spoonful of gravy. Top with the salad and enjoy immediately.

Christmas Beef Tenderloin

10 TO 12 SERVINGS

In my family, we don't do Christmas Eve without beef tenderloin. This marinade was given to my mom by a friend years ago, and although I am not typically a fan of marinades for beef, this one is a giant exception. There's something magnificent about the display of a whole beef tenderloin, and its delicate, rich flavor always lives up to the hype.

1 cup [240 ml] olive oil

1 cup [240 ml] soy sauce

¾ cup [180 ml] red wine vinegar

½ cup [120 ml] fresh lemon juice

¼ cup [60 ml] Worcestershire sauce

3 garlic cloves, chopped

3 Tbsp dry mustard

1 Tbsp dried parsley

1 Tbsp freshly ground black pepper

1 Tbsp salt

1 beef tenderloin, trimmed, rinsed, and patted dry

In a large roasting pan or deep dish, mix together the olive oil, soy sauce, vinegar, lemon juice, Worcestershire sauce, garlic, dry mustard, parsley, black pepper, and salt. Place the tenderloin in the marinade mixture, turning to coat. Cover and refrigerate for at least 24 hours or up to 4 days.

Remove the tenderloin from the marinade and let rest on the counter at room temperature for 45 minutes. Grill the tenderloin on a barbecue directly over moderately high heat, or on the stovetop in a grilling pan over medium-high heat, turning often, until nicely charred, about 30 minutes for medium-rare. Transfer to a carving board and let rest for 20 minutes. Slice ½ in [12 mm] thick and serve immediately, or store in an airtight container in the refrigerator for up to 4 days.

No. 7

ts & stries

Rosemary Focaccia

10 TO 12 SERVINGS

This was one of the very first recipes I learned in pastry, and I fell in love with it because it's so damn practical. It's easy to follow, it doesn't require a biga (the traditional Italian starter dough) or other yeast starter, and it isn't finicky like standard loaf recipes are. This is the ideal bread to attempt from home. You can start three hours before your party and guests will be greeted by the smell of fresh bread, making you look like the hostess goddess that you are. You're welcome.

One ¼ oz [7 g] package active dry yeast

1 tsp sugar

½ cup [120 ml] olive oil

5½ cups [685 g] all-purpose flour, plus more as needed

2 tsp salt

¼ cup [5 g] chopped, fresh rosemary

In a stand mixer with the dough hook attached, whisk together the yeast, sugar, and 1½ cups [350 ml] of warm water. Let the yeast mixture sit for at least 10 minutes while measuring out the remaining ingredients individually in bowls.

After 10 minutes, and once the yeast is slightly foamy, turn the mixer to low speed. Add ¼ cup [60 ml] of the olive oil, the flour, and 1 tsp of the salt and mix until combined, 3 to 4 minutes. Add half of the rosemary, then turn the mixer to medium-high speed and let knead for 5 to 8 minutes or up to 20 minutes until the dough is smooth, slightly sticky, and pulling away from the sides, forming a loose ball around the hook. If it is not pulling away from the sides, add another ¼ cup [30 g] of flour and continue mixing.

Turn the dough out onto a cutting board and shape it into a ball. Oil a large mixing bowl with 1 Tbsp of the olive oil and place the dough in the bowl. Loosely cover the bowl with a damp tea towel and set in a warm area (such as on your dryer or near the oven or, on a warm day, a window) and let it rise until doubled in size, 45 minutes to 1 hour.

cont'd

Preheat the oven to 400°F [205°C]. Oil a standard half sheet pan with 1 Tbsp of the olive oil. Place the dough in the pan, pushing and pressing from the middle until the dough has stretched to the sides. Cover the dough with an oiled piece of plastic wrap and let rise for another 20 minutes.

Remove the plastic wrap and use your fingertips to press deep dimples all over the dough surface down to the pan. Evenly drizzle the surface with 1 Tbsp of the olive oil and sprinkle the remaining rosemary and the remaining 1 tsp of salt over the top.

Bake for 15 to 20 minutes, or until the dough is golden and cooked throughout. Remove from the oven, let sit for 20 minutes, then cut and serve warm with the remaining 1 Tbsp of olive oil on the side.

VARIATION   Grape and Fennel Focaccia

2 cups [240 g] green or red grapes, halved vertically

2 cups [200 g] slivered fennel

¼ cup [60 ml] olive oil

In a small bowl, toss together the grapes, fennel, and olive oil. Evenly spread the mixture over the focaccia dough right before baking. Follow the remaining directions for Rosemary Focaccia (left).

Corn-Mold Skillet Cornbread

12 TO 15 SERVINGS

When my grandmother passed, her two corn-mold skillets and one triangle loaf skillet were given to me. She made cornbread often and always used these pans. When I made it to the *Top Chef* finals, we were given two weeks to decompress from the first phase of competition in Kentucky and prepare for the next phase, which would take place in Macau, China. In that time, we also had to plan our finale meal in detail—in case we made it that far—down to the complete ingredient list. The only tip we were given was to "plan the meal of your life, as if your life depended on it." No pressure.

I'd poured myself into each challenge and had used a lot of my favorite recipes already. Leaving Kentucky, I had no clue what I'd use in my finale menu. To my delight and relief, however, when I returned home in the thick of Alabama summer, I was completely inspired by my favorite season in the South. One afternoon, as I reminisced about my grandparents and their love for the classic Southern combination of buttermilk and cornbread, my menu was born.

When I boarded the plane for Macau, my suitcase held my grandmother's corn-mold skillets and four cornmeal varieties. They traveled with me across the world by plane, ferry, and bus. To say this recipe, in these molds, is important to me is an understatement.

3 cups [375 g] all-purpose flour

2 cups [260 g] fine ground yellow cornmeal

¼ cup [50 g] sugar

1 Tbsp baking powder

1 tsp baking soda

1 tsp salt

1½ cups [345 g] unsalted butter, cold, cut into tablespoon-size cubes, plus more for greasing the skillet

1 cup [240 ml] buttermilk

1 egg, beaten, for egg wash

Preheat the oven to 350°F [175°C]. In a stand mixer with a paddle attachment, combine the flour, cornmeal, sugar, baking powder, baking soda, salt, and butter. Mix on low speed until the butter has broken down to the size of peas. Gradually add the buttermilk, stopping the mixer midway to scrape the sides and bottom of the bowl; mix until just combined. Remove the paddle attachment and use a rubber spatula to gently fold the dough from the bottom, being sure all the dry ingredients have been incorporated.

Grease a corn-mold skillet, standard large skillet, or regular muffin tins. Fill the skillet or tins three-quarters of the way with the dough, gently pressing the top to flatten. Using a pastry brush, brush the top with the egg wash. Bake for 8 to 10 minutes for corn molds or muffins or 15 to 20 minutes for a large skillet, or until golden and a toothpick comes out clean. Remove the skillet from the oven, let it sit on a towel for 10 minutes, then invert the cornbread onto a cooling rack. Serve warm.

OG Buttermilk Biscuits

4 BISCUITS

If you needed to describe Southern cooking in two words, *buttermilk* and *biscuits* would suffice. Put 'em together and you may as well just throw a hoedown. That said, when we had biscuits when I was growing up, they were out of a can. I didn't realize just how hard they were to perfect until I decided to put a biscuit bar on the brunch menu at KBC to honor my husband's grandmother Mimi. She was the kind of woman who made biscuits every mornin' and was famous for them. I aspire to follow in her footsteps.

For months, I overworked, under-worked, added too much, added too little, baked too long, baked too little, until one day, I did it. I made the most perfect, fluffy, layered, decadent batch of biscuits! Turns out, it was the first recipe I ever tried—sort of like that first wedding dress—and ended up being what I now refer to as the OG Buttermilk Biscuit recipe. There're a lot of ways to make a biscuit, but to make a great biscuit, you've got to relax and can't overthink it.

Today, biscuits are my favorite thing to make and my favorite thing to teach people to make. I've done all the overthinking for you already, so to make a gold-standard biscuit, all you need to do is get out a rolling pin and follow this recipe to a T.

2 cups [250 g] all-purpose flour, plus more for dusting

1 Tbsp baking powder

1 tsp salt

½ tsp sugar

½ cup [115 g] unsalted butter, cubed, ice cold

¾ cup [180 ml] buttermilk, ice cold

1 egg, beaten

Honey Butter and Quick Jam (recipes follow), for serving

Preheat the oven to 450°F [220°C]. Line a sheet pan with parchment paper. In a large bowl, whisk together the flour, baking powder, salt, and sugar. Scatter the butter over the flour mixture and freeze for 20 minutes. This ensures that the bowl and ingredients are good and cold.

Remove the flour and butter mixture from the freezer and shake it into a food processor fitted with the blade attachment. Pulse until the mixture resembles coarse crumbs the size of small peas (about 10 pulses). Pour the mixture back into the cold bowl.

Using a spoon, dig a small crater in the middle of the mixture. Pour the buttermilk into the crater. With a wooden or metal spoon, gently stir until just combined, forming a shaggy dough. Your dough should just barely come together, leaving at least ¼ cup [30 g] of flour mix in the bottom of the bowl.

Dust a flat surface with flour by sifting over it. (The benefit of sifted flour is it prevents sticking but isn't incorporated into the dough.) Turn the dough out onto the floured surface and knead gently and quickly to form a ball.

cont'd

With a rolling pin, roll the dough out to ¼ in [6 mm] thickness, shaping it into a long oval. (The dough will be roughly the same height as your flat hand on the surface of the table.) Fold the dough top to bottom like an envelope and press with your fingertips, making sure the two sides are sealed together. Repeat this step, folding left to right. Your dough should now be in the shape of a square. Flip the dough over and sift more flour on top. Roll out the dough to ½ in [12 mm] thickness. (The dough will now be as thick as both your hands stacked on top of one another on the table.) Using a sharp knife, cut the biscuits into four even squares, making sure to cut every side. Or use a 3 in [8 cm] round ring cutter or an empty soup can to cut out the biscuits by pressing straight down. Don't turn the cutter—that will cause the edges to seal, preventing them from rising to perfection.

Place the biscuits 2 in [5 cm] apart on the prepared sheet. Brush evenly and lightly with the egg wash. Bake for 10 to 12 minutes, or until golden brown. Let cool for about 10 minutes, then enjoy immediately.

Honey Butter
—— 4 TO 6 SERVINGS OR ½ CUP [115 G] BUTTER

½ cup [115 g] butter, at room temperature

3 Tbsp honey

¼ tsp salt

In a small bowl, stir together the ingredients until combined; spread on each half of a warm biscuit. The honey butter will

keep in an airtight container in the refrigerator for up to 3 months.

Quick Jam
—— 4 TO 6 SERVINGS OR 2 CUPS [700 G] JAM

4 cups [500 g] mixed fresh or frozen berries

2 cups [400 g] sugar

Zest and juice of 1 lemon

In a large saucepan, combine all the ingredients. Bring to a simmer over medium-low heat, stirring constantly. Lower the heat to low and continue to simmer, halfway off the heat, for 20 to 30 minutes. Stir frequently, making sure the bottom does not burn. The jam should be thick but not stiff. To test the consistency, spread a thin line of jam on your counter or a cold plate. The jam should easily hold a firm edge when spread with a spoon and have a slightly wrinkled texture. Enjoy immediately, or follow the Canning 101 procedure (page 34).

⇢ MIMI'S ⇠ BISCUIT BAR

Here are some favorite variations I urge y'all to try.

KBC CHICKEN BISCUIT
Bee's Fried Chicken (page 181), Pimiento Cheese (page 59), bacon

SUNRISE BISCUIT
Sausage, bacon, Pimiento Cheese (page 59), fried egg

BACK ROADS BISCUIT
Country ham, smoked Gouda, bacon, fried egg

ALABAMA BENEDICT
Hot sauce hollandaise, fried ham, sunny-side-up egg

Golf Cart Cinnamon Rolls

2 DOZEN ROLLS

My mom is a master of traditions—most of which revolve around food. When we were growing up, our holiday meals were as sacred to her as our suppertime blessings. What I know of them now is part generations-old tradition and part modern ingenuity—the mark of a strong and smart Southern woman.

On Christmas Eve, my cousins would come to town and we'd start right in on the prep for Christmas morning. Our favorite part was helping our moms with the cinnamon roll dough. It was magic that this bowl of flour, sugar, and yeast would turn into such a delectable treat overnight. We'd let the dough rise, carefully roll out the logs, and put them in the fridge. The next morning, we'd wake up early to see what Santa had brought and equally importantly, put our buns in the oven. While they rose to pillowy perfection, we'd make the cream cheese icing, grits, and breakfast casserole and pack it up to share at our neighbors'.

In 2003, we wished (more like begged and pleaded) for a shared golf cart. When we were fortunate enough to find it waiting in the driveway on Christmas morning, we were thrilled to have wheels to deliver all our goodies. We loaded it up and made sure one of the cousins held on tight to the cinnamon rolls. I can still hear our moms hollerin' at us as we drove off, threatening our lives if we dropped those beloved rolls. All it took was one sharp turn and—you guessed it—the rolls ended up in a hot steaming pile on the turf. We knew that if our moms found out, we'd never see that golf cart again. So we did what any good child would do. We brushed them off, shaped them back together, and prayed for dear life we wouldn't get caught.

We still have the golf cart. Sorry, Mom.

FOR THE DOUGH

4 Tbsp [58 g] unsalted butter, at room temperature, plus ½ cup [115 g], melted, and more for greasing the bowl

1 cup [240 ml] whole milk

Two ¼ oz [7 g] packages active dry yeast

½ cup [100 g] plus 1 Tbsp granulated sugar

2 eggs

2 Tbsp lemon zest (about 1 lemon's worth; use the juice for the icing)

2 tsp salt

1 tsp vanilla extract

½ tsp nutmeg

½ tsp cinnamon

6 cups [750 g] all-purpose flour, plus more for dusting

FOR THE FILLING

2 cups [200 g] pecans, chopped

1½ cups [255 g] light brown sugar

5 Tbsp [30 g] cinnamon

1 tsp nutmeg

FOR THE ICING

2 cups [250 g] confectioners' sugar

8 oz [225 g] cream cheese, at room temperature

½ cup [115 g] unsalted butter, at room temperature

1 tsp vanilla extract

1 tsp fresh lemon juice (use the lemon you zested!)

cont'd

To make the dough: In a small sauce-pan, melt the 4 Tbsp [58 g] of room-temperature butter. Add the milk and heat until warm but not hot. Set aside. In a small bowl, mix together the yeast, ⅔ cup [158 ml] of warm water, and 1 Tbsp of the granulated sugar. Set aside.

In a stand mixer with the paddle attachment, mix together the remaining ½ cup [100 g] of granulated sugar and the milk mixture on low speed until smooth. Add the yeast mixture and the eggs, lemon zest, salt, vanilla, nutmeg, and cinnamon. Replace the paddle with the dough hook. On low speed, slowly incorporate the flour. Continue to mix until a ball forms and pulls away from the sides of the bowl, about 8 minutes.

Remove the dough and knead it into a ball. Butter a large bowl, place the dough in the bowl, and roll the dough around to coat with butter. Wrap the bowl tightly in plastic wrap or tie a small garbage bag around to make it airtight. Keep in a warm place for about 1½ hours or until the dough doubles in size.

To make the filling: While the dough is rising, mix together the pecans, brown sugar, cinnamon, and nutmeg. Set aside.

To make the icing: In a stand mixer with the whisk attachment, beat the confectioners' sugar, cream cheese, butter, vanilla, and lemon juice together until smooth. Refrigerate in a tightly sealed container. When the rolls go into the oven, take the icing out of the refrigerator so it can come to room temperature while the rolls bake.

To assemble: Once the dough has doubled, it's time to fill and roll. Lightly flour a work surface and roll out the dough ½ in [12 mm] thick and roughly 25 in [64 cm] long by 10 in [25 cm] wide. Use a pastry brush to lightly coat with the ½ cup [115 g] of melted butter.

Sprinkle the filling mixture evenly over the dough, leaving a ½ in [12 mm] clean margin on each side. Tightly roll the dough, pulling back as you roll. Pinch the dough to seal and then roll to smooth out the seam. Using a serrated bread knife, cut the log into 24 slices about 1 in [2.5 cm] wide.

Heavily butter two 9 by 13 in [23 by 33 cm] casserole dishes. Evenly arrange the rolls in the dishes; they should be touching. Drape a thin towel, such as linen, over the buns and place in a warm area to let the dough double in size again, about 45 minutes.

When the rolls have about 10 minutes of rising time left, preheat the oven to 350°F [175°C]. Bake for 25 minutes, or until golden brown. Let cool to room temperature, then spread the icing over the top, and serve.

➤ NOTE ◀

BEST CASE
You have all the time in the world (and the ingredients) to make the icing recipe.

HACK
Mix together 2 cups [250 g] confectioners' sugar, 2 Tbsp melted unsalted butter, 1 tsp vanilla extract, and 1 Tbsp milk to make a quick sweet glaze. Bonus: Replace the milk with orange juice and you've got orange sweet rolls.

219

Banana Nut Bread

2 LOAVES

This is not bread; it is cake. My mom made this when our bananas would go bad—and by bad I mean black banana peels. It's a simple recipe that feels homey and warm. It's something you can whip up on a weekday afternoon, or enjoy for breakfast. And who doesn't like cake you can eat for breakfast?

3 cups [375 g] all-purpose flour, plus more for dusting the pans

2 tsp baking soda

1 tsp salt

5 bananas, very ripe

2 cups [400 g] sugar

½ cup [115 g] shortening

½ cup [115 g] unsalted butter, at room temperature, plus more for greasing the pans

4 eggs

6 Tbsp buttermilk

2 tsp vanilla extract

1 cup [100 g] pecans, chopped

Preheat the oven to 325°F [165°C]. Grease and flour two 9 by 5 in [23 by 12 cm] loaf pans.

In a medium mixing bowl, combine the flour, baking soda, and salt and set aside. In a stand mixer with the paddle attachment, beat the bananas with the sugar, shortening, and butter on medium-high speed until whipped and creamy, 5 to 7 minutes. Add the eggs, one at a time, then the buttermilk and vanilla; mix until incorporated.

With the mixer on low speed, add the flour mixture in three batches. Stop midway to scrape the sides of the bowl with a rubber spatula. Mix until combined. Remove the bowl from the mixer and fold in the pecans. Pour the batter into the prepared pans and bake for 50 to 60 minutes, or until the tops are golden and a toothpick comes out clean. Let cool for 10 minutes before inverting onto a cooling rack. Let cool for at least another 10 to 15 minutes before slicing. Enjoy warm or at room temperature.

Muffin Base

1 DOZEN JUMBO, 2 DOZEN REGULAR, OR 3 DOZEN MINI MUFFINS

My favorite thing about this muffin recipe is its versatility. I love, love, love a blank canvas recipe that allows you to be the artist, and this one is just that. When I worked in fine dining pastry, I realized baking was all about ratios and techniques, and I became fixated on the creation of base recipes. Rather than having twelve ice cream recipes, five cake recipes, and ten cookie recipes, I came to the realization that you could have *one* really amazing, really per-fect base recipe that could be easily altered. This muffin recipe was the test case that proved my theory. I get you started with an herb and citrus favorite of mine, but you can add any-thing to this base and the muffins will taste amazing. Scout's honor.

3 cups [375 g] all-purpose flour

2 cups [400 g] sugar

1 Tbsp baking powder

1 tsp baking soda

¼ tsp salt

1½ cups [345 g] unsalted butter, cold, cut into tablespoon-size cubes

1½ cups [360 g] sour cream

3 large eggs plus 2 large egg yolks

2 tsp vanilla extract

Preheat the oven to 375°F [190°C] and line muffin tins with paper cups.

In a stand mixer with the paddle attachment, mix together the flour, sugar, baking powder, baking soda, salt, and butter on medium-low speed for 3 to 4 minutes, or until the butter bits are about the size of frozen peas. Remove the bowl from the mixer and, using a rubber spatula, fold in the sour cream, eggs, yolks, and vanilla. Fold in any desired additions.

Bake for 12 to 15 minutes for jumbo, 10 to 12 min-utes for regular, or 8 to 10 minutes for mini muffins, or until the tops are golden and a toothpick comes out clean. Store muffins in an airtight container at room temperature for up to 3 days.

cont'd

Orange Thyme Muffins with Orange Icing

—— 1 DOZEN JUMBO, 2 DOZEN REGULAR,
OR 3 DOZEN MINI MUFFINS

2 sprigs thyme

Zest and juice of 3 oranges

Muffin Base (page 221)

2 cups [350 g] confectioners' sugar

Pull the thyme leaves from the stems and finely chop. Add the zest and juice of 2 oranges and the thyme into the muffin base and bake as directed. While the muffins are baking, in a small bowl, whisk together the remaining zest and juice with the confectioners' sugar. When the muffins have cooled, drizzle the icing over the tops and allow to set for 10 minutes.

These variations are my favorites to date. Have fun coming up with your own signature add-ins.

1 cup [125 g] cubed peaches, tossed in flour + ½ tsp cinnamon

1 cup [190 g] berries, tossed in flour + 1 Tbsp fresh lemon juice + 1 Tbsp lemon zest

¼ cup [30 g] poppy seeds + 2 Tbsp fresh lemon or orange juice

1 cup [160 g] chocolate chips + ½ cup [50 g] nuts

Beeb's Blackberry Cobbler

Beeb was my great-grandmother Lil's little sister. She was a consummate baker, and many of my great-grandmother's pastry recipes came from her. This is a classic batter cobbler recipe that can be made with just about any fruit filling. I dare you to find one that isn't appealing.

1 cup [125 g] all-purpose flour

1 cup [200 g] plus 2 Tbsp sugar

1 Tbsp baking powder

Pinch of salt

¾ cup [180 ml] whole milk

½ cup [115 g] unsalted butter, melted

4 cups [500 g] fresh blackberries (or blueberries, strawberries, cherries, or raspberries)

1 tsp fresh lemon juice

Vanilla ice cream, for serving

Preheat the oven to 350°F [175°C]. In a medium mixing bowl, sift the flour, 1 cup [200 g] of the sugar, the baking powder, and salt, then whisk in the milk.

In an 8 by 8 in [20 by 20 cm] baking pan, 9 by 9 in [23 by 23 cm] baking pan, or 9 in [23 cm] pie plate, pour the melted butter, then pour the batter. Evenly disperse the berries over the batter and sprinkle with the remaining 2 Tbsp of sugar and the lemon juice.

Bake for 20 to 30 minutes, or until bubbling and golden brown. Serve warm with vanilla ice cream.

Icebox Cookies

1 DOZEN LARGE COOKIES

Old friends who've seen you at your worst and, most importantly, have stood beside you through it all are absolute treasures. There are three in particular with whom I share a unique bond. Allie I met during rush at Auburn University. She got a fan stuck in her hair right before we walked into the first sorority house, and we both cried laughing trying to get it out. Leigh I met the second week of college at our Chi O pledge retreat. She was vocal and passionate about her political views, and I knew we'd get along. Jessica and I befriended each other when I realized we both had an affinity for arguing and a feistiness that could not be tempered.

We are each strong, confident, and career-driven. We have also muddled through our share of personal drama. In college, whenever we'd have a "crisis," we'd drop everything and meet at Leigh's apartment. I always made cookie dough, and we'd eat it straight out of the bowl. I quickly learned to have this emergency provision on hand, and I began storing it in the freezer. We ate a lot of cookie dough during those college years. Though we don't live within walking distance anymore, we still get together often, and I still make these cookies. It's a decade later and our friendship seems to get sweeter every year.

1 cup [230 g] unsalted butter, at room temperature

1 cup [170 g] light brown sugar

½ cup [100 g] granulated sugar

1 tsp vanilla extract

2 eggs

2½ cups [315 g] all-purpose flour

2 tsp salt

1 tsp baking soda

Additions of your choice (variations follow)

In a large bowl, using an electric mixer on medium-high speed, beat the butter, brown sugar, granulated sugar, and vanilla until well combined and light yellow in color, about 2 minutes. Gradually add the eggs.

In a separate bowl, combine the flour, salt, and baking soda.

Slowly add the flour mixture to the wet ingredients and beat on low speed until well incorporated. Fold in any additions with a rubber spatula or wooden spoon.

Preheat the oven to 325°F [165°C]. Line a baking sheet with parchment paper.

Scoop the dough onto the baking sheet with a 4 oz [115 g] self-scrape ice cream scooper. Using a scoop ensures a consistent size—big, that is! Gently press the dough balls to flatten slightly—about 1 in [2.5 cm] thick—and freeze the dough for 20 minutes before baking. Bake for 12 to 14 minutes, or until golden brown, turning the sheet halfway through.

cont'd

The dough can be refrigerated in a ziplock bag or airtight container for up to 5 days or frozen for up to 6 months.

VARIATIONS

Cornflake–Chocolate Chip Cookies

1½ cups [50 g] cornflakes

1 cup [160 g] chocolate chips

Samoa Cookies

1½ cups [150 g] unsweetened shredded coconut

1 cup [160 g] chocolate chips

1 cup [160 g] Heath bar pieces

German Chocolate Cookies

1 cup [160 g] chocolate chips

1 cup [100 g] unsweetened shredded coconut

1 cup [100 g] chopped pecans

Double Chocolate Cookies

1 cup [160 g] chocolate chips

Substitute ½ cup [62 g] cocoa powder for ½ cup [65 g] of the all-purpose flour

Oatmeal Nut Cookies

1 cup [100 g] oatmeal

½ cup [50 g] chopped walnuts

½ cup [50 g] chopped pecans

1 tsp cinnamon

Red Velvet Cookies

1 cup [160 g] white chocolate chunks

2 Tbsp red food coloring

1 Tbsp cocoa powder

······· NOTE ·······

I make a quadruple batch of this dough and keep it in the freezer for those moments when I just "need it." Let it thaw and have kids add their own toppings for a quick afternoon playdate, or invite your best girls over for cookies and cocktails. No work and all win on your part.

Key Lime Crunch

15 TO 20 SERVINGS

This recipe began as a joke on *Top Chef*. I was notoriously anxious about the Quickfire Challenges. I had a deep fear that I'd choke and have produced nothing when it was my turn to face the judges. Early in the season, late one night around the dinner table, I told some of the chefs that if all else failed, I'd make "Puppy Chow." I was met with puzzled looks. This chocolate peanut butter cereal snack, which I'd thought was popular among teenage girlfriends everywhere, is apparently not a universal confection. I had to explain this addictive, stupidly simple snack to this group of top-notch chefs, and of course they all challenged me to do it in the next Quickfire.

Fast-forward a few weeks, and this little joke became a national reality. I made Key Lime Crunch—a riff on "Puppy Chow"—as a party favor to send our houseboat party over the top. We won as a team, I won the challenge, and this lives on. It's a can't-stop-once-you-start snack that is sure to put a smile on your guests' faces. If you don't believe me, just ask Emeril.

5 cups [800 g] white chocolate chips

Zest and juice of 5 limes

4 cups [140 g] Chex cereal (any variety)

4 cups [140 g] Cinnamon Life cereal

3 cups [105 g] Honey Bunches of Oats cereal

1 cup [125 g] macadamia nuts, whole or halved

1 cup [130 g] cashews, whole or halved

1 cup [80 g] banana chips

1 cup [100 g] shredded coconut

3 Tbsp salt

Zest of 2 lemons

One 14 oz [400 g] box graham crackers, crumbled

In a large mixing bowl, melt the white chocolate. Place 1 cup [160 g] of the melted chocolate in a small bowl and whisk in the lime juice. It will seize; that's OK!

Line two sheet pans with parchment paper. In a very large bowl or tub, toss together all the cereals, the macadamia nuts, cashews, banana chips, coconut, 1½ Tbsp of the salt, and the lemon zest. Pour the lime and chocolate mixture and the remaining melted chocolate over the top and toss together thoroughly. Promptly pour the mixture onto the prepared pans. Separate and flatten the mixture so there are no large clumps. Sprinkle with the graham cracker crumbs, remaining 1½ Tbsp of salt, and the lime zest. Let sit out for about 1 hour or until the chocolate has hardened. Gently break up into bite-size pieces before serving.

Classic Pie Dough

TWO 9 IN [23 CM] PIECRUSTS

When it comes to dough, I love butter, and I believe in homemade. I'd be lying if I said I never bought a store-bought shell (I even suggest it in this book, for those times when you're in a pinch), but I urge you to at least *try* the homemade route. I'd also love to ask you to teach your children, your neighbor's children, your sister's children (OK, any children) how to make it from scratch. I'd like to say that I'm the initiator of the "Keep Homemade Pie Alive" movement, and I urge you to join me in this mission. Sincerely, Kelsey Barnard Clark.

1 cup [230 g] unsalted butter, cut into tablespoon-size cubes

3 cups [375 g] all-purpose flour, plus more for dusting

1 Tbsp sugar

1 tsp salt

6 to 8 Tbsp [90 to 120 ml] ice water

In a medium mixing bowl, add the butter and flour and place it in the freezer for 20 minutes. Flour a work surface well. Remove the mixture from the freezer and transfer it to a food processor fitted with the blade attachment. Add the sugar and salt and pulse 8 to 12 times, until the butter is the size of frozen peas.

As you continue pulsing, pour the ice water down the feed tube, a bit at a time, until the dough begins to form a ball. Turn the dough out onto the floured work surface and quickly roll it into a ball, being sure not to handle it too much with your hands. Wrap the dough tightly in plastic wrap and refrigerate for 30 minutes, or freeze, wrapped, for up to 6 months. If frozen, let thaw for 1 hour before continuing to the next step.

cont'd

231

Unwrap the dough and cut it in half. On a well-floured surface, use a rolling pin to flatten and roll each piece into a circular disk, rolling from the center to the edge, turning and flouring the dough to make sure it doesn't stick to the surface. Roll out the dough until it is at least 1 in [2.5 cm] wider than the pie dish. Place your rolling pin in the middle of the dough round, fold the dough in half over the pin, and transfer it to the pie dish, unfolding it to fit the dish. The dough should ease into the dish without stretching or pulling. Using a sharp paring knife or kitchen shears, trim the excess dough to the rim of the dish. Crimp the edge or press with a fork. Freeze for 15 to 20 minutes to chill before blind-baking. Cover the other rolled-out piece of dough and keep refrigerated until you're ready to fill and bake the pie.

To blind-bake the piecrust, preheat the oven to 400°F [205°C]. Remove the prepared pie shell from the freezer and line it with parchment paper, crumpling up the paper first to be sure that it easily shapes inside the crust. Fill the shell halfway with dried beans or pie weights. Bake until the edges are golden, 15 to 18 minutes. Remove the shell from the oven and carefully lift the parchment paper and weights out of the shell. Return the shell to the oven for 6 to 8 minutes to slightly brown the bottom for classic blind baking or for 14 to 15 minutes for a no-bake pie (such as Banana Cream Pie, page 234).

◾ NOTE ◾

All-butter versus shortening crust: Although shortening has a higher melting point than butter, making it easier to handle and roll out, it lacks the flavor that butter boasts and often leaves a greasy film in your mouth. Freezing the flour and butter together before handling prevents it from melting and creates a velvety, flaky crust.

Don't skip the last step, in which you freeze the prepared shell briefly before blind-baking. This prevents the piecrust from shrinking and is the most important step.

Mama Jo's Pecan Pie

ONE 9 IN [23 CM] PIE

I dearly loved my grandmother and appreciated all of her qualities, but doting and pampering were not exactly in her wheelhouse. For that, we had Mama Jo, my mom's best friend's mother. We sometimes ate at her house after church, and sometimes she'd skip church altogether just to prepare dumplings, deviled eggs, pear salad, and fried cornbread for her family (and ours).

My dad considers himself a pecan pie connoisseur, and upon his first bite of her buttery pie, he deemed her the queen. I have to agree with him. This pie is packed with pecans and has a rich brown-butter flavor.

3 eggs

1 cup [200 g] sugar

1 cup [240 ml] light corn syrup

½ cup [115 g] unsalted butter, browned, then cooled

1 tsp vanilla extract

¼ tsp fresh lemon juice

¼ tsp salt

1½ cups [150 g] raw pecan halves

One 9 in [23 cm] pie shell, blind-baked (see Classic Pie Dough, page 231)

Preheat the oven to 400°F [205°C]. In a stand mixer with whisk attachment, beat the eggs and sugar on medium-high speed until light and slightly foamy. Add the corn syrup, browned butter, vanilla, lemon juice, and salt and mix on medium speed until completely combined. Layer the pecans in the prepared pie shell and pour the syrup mixture over the pecans. Pat the pecans down with a spoon, making sure they are all coated. Bake in the middle rack of the oven for 10 minutes, then lower the temperature to 325°F [165°C] and bake for 35 to 45 minutes, or until set in the middle and golden on top. Cool for 2 to 4 hours before serving at room temperature.

Banana Cream Pie

ONE 9 IN [23 CM] PIE

This was my mom's favorite treat growing up. While in college at the University of South Alabama, she often would drive to my great-grandmother Lil and Grandaddy Cocky's house for lunch. More often than not, the centerpiece was my great-grandmother's banana cream pie. It's the perfect balance of sweet and creamy, unassuming and humble. It happens to be one of my very favorite desserts as well—I guess even taste buds are genetic.

FOR THE WHIPPED CREAM

2 Tbsp confectioners' sugar

1 tsp vanilla extract

2 cups [480 ml] heavy whipping cream, ice cold

FOR THE FILLING

One 8 oz [225 g] package cream cheese, at room temperature

One 14 oz [420 ml] can sweetened condensed milk

⅓ cup [80 ml] fresh lemon juice

1 tsp vanilla extract

3 bananas, sliced into ½ in [12 mm] rounds

One 9 in [23 cm] pie shell, prebaked (see Classic Pie Dough, page 231)

To make the whipped cream: In a chilled mixing bowl, combine the sugar and vanilla on medium-high speed, then add the whipping cream. Dampen a tea towel and drape it over the stand mixer and bowl, creating a tent around the bowl. Whip the cream, holding the towel around the bowl (to catch spatters), until the cream reaches stiff peaks, 2 to 3 minutes. Scrape the whipped cream out into a medium mixing bowl and set aside.

To make the filling: In the same stand mixer bowl (no need to wash it out), whisk the cream cheese on medium-high speed until light and fluffy, 2 to 3 minutes. Turn the speed down to medium-low and slowly add the condensed milk, mixing until well blended. Continue running the mixer and add the lemon juice and vanilla until well blended.

To assemble: Evenly place the banana slices in the baked and cooled pie shell and pour the filling over the bananas. Evenly top with the whipped cream. Refrigerate for 2 hours until firm, then enjoy cool.

234

Key Lime Pie

ONE 9 IN [23 CM] PIE

This is my husband's very favorite dessert. To be honest, I can't say I was ever really that fond of this tart pie until we got together. It is a Southern classic that I somehow bypassed for much of my life that now frequently reminds me of my favorite "pre-children" memory with him. When we were engaged and then newlyweds, I'd often have to work at the beach on Saturday nights catering weddings. He typically would join me and manage the bar for the event. We'd spend Sundays on the beach sipping ice-cold beer and visiting our favorite local spots, where we'd enjoy a slow, relaxed, lazy lunch that almost always ended with a slice of key lime pie. These days, our lunches out are anything but relaxed, with bites of food quickly shoved into our mouths in between feeding, coddling, and doing our damnedest to quiet one of our littles. Sometimes I order a slice—more often than not, to go—and just have to laugh at the difference a few years can make. I'm certain in twenty years we'll be having quiet key lime pie lunches once again and we'll be missing these hectic lunches more than ever.

FOR THE GRAHAM CRACKER CRUST

2 cups [150 g] graham crackers

5 Tbsp [70 g] unsalted butter, melted

⅓ cup [66 g] granulated sugar

FOR THE FILLING

3 egg yolks

2 tsp lime zest

One 14 oz [420 ml] can sweetened condensed milk

⅔ cup [160 ml] fresh key lime juice (can substitute with regular limes)

FOR THE WHIPPED CREAM

2 cups [480 ml] heavy whipping cream, ice cold

2 Tbsp confectioners' sugar

1 tsp vanilla extract

To make the crust: Preheat the oven to 350°F [175°C]. In a food processer, process the graham crackers until they are mostly smooth crumbs. If you don't have a food processor, place the crackers in a large plastic bag, seal, and crush the crackers with a rolling pin. Add the melted butter and granulated sugar to the cracker crumbs and pulse or stir until combined. Press the mixture into the bottom and sides of a 9 in [23 cm] pie pan, forming a neat border around the edge. Bake the crust until set and golden, about 8 minutes. Set on a cooling rack to cool and leave the oven on.

cont'd

To make the filling: Using an electric mixer with the wire whisk attachment, beat the egg yolks and lime zest on high speed until light and very fluffy, about 5 minutes. Gradually add the condensed milk and continue to beat until thick, 3 or 4 minutes longer. Lower the speed to medium-low and slowly add the lime juice, mixing until just combined, 1 minute max. Pour the mixture into the crust. Bake for 10 minutes or until the filling has set. Cool on a wire rack for 10 minutes, then refrigerate for 45 minutes or up to 4 days to set.

To make the whipped cream: In a chilled mixing bowl, combine the whipping cream, confectioners' sugar, and vanilla. Dampen a tea towel and drape it over the stand mixer and bowl, creating a tent around the bowl. Whip the cream on medium-high speed, holding the towel around the bowl (to catch any spatters), until the cream reaches stiff peaks, 2 to 3 minutes.

Serve the pie very cold, cut into wedges, each topped with a large dollop of whipped cream.

Mrs. Rodman's Cream Cheese Pound Cake

10 TO 12 SERVINGS

Mrs. Rodman lived across the street from us growing up. She was a sweet, gentle old woman who loved to bake. She was in my parents' Bible study class (for which her husband always donned a bow tie, hand-stitched by her). Every Sunday, she brought a warm pound cake, fresh out of the oven, with silky ribbons of butter throughout and the most perfect caramelized crust. My mom begged her for her recipe and, eventually, she kindly obliged. To this day, I follow her directions, written in cursive scroll on a church bulletin.

Over the years, I've also developed a variation for chocolate lovers. We use the original and the chocolate versions layered with cream cheese frosting for birthday cakes at KBC. No matter how you slice it, this cake is foolproof and tastes like a little piece of heaven.

1½ cups [345 g] unsalted butter, at room temperature

One 8 oz [225 g] package cream cheese, at room temperature

3 cups [600 g] sugar

6 eggs

3 cups [375 g] all-purpose flour

1 Tbsp vanilla extract

¼ tsp salt

Preheat the oven to 325°F [165°C]. Grease and flour one 10 cup [2.3 L] Bundt pan, two 9 by 5 in [23 by 12 cm] loaf pans, or three 8 in [20 cm] round cake pans.

In a stand mixer with the paddle attachment, beat together the butter, cream cheese, and sugar on medium speed until light and fluffy, 8 to 10 minutes, turning off the mixer midway to scrape the sides of the bowl. With the mixer on medium-low speed, add the eggs, one at a time, letting each incorporate before adding the next. Next, add the flour in three batches, scraping the sides of the bowl midway through. Add the vanilla and salt and mix to incorporate. Pour into the prepared pan(s).

Bake for 60 to 90 minutes for a Bundt, 45 to 60 minutes for loaves, or 30 to 45 minutes for cake layers. The cake is done when the top is golden and a toothpick comes out clean. Remove the pan from the oven and let the cake rest on a towel for 10 minutes, then invert it onto a cooling rack. Let cool for 20 minutes before cutting. Serve warm or at room temperature but do *not* refrigerate.

cont'd

Cream Cheese Frosting
—— 6 CUPS [1.2 KG]

Two 8 oz [450 g] packages cream cheese, at room temperature

1 cup [230 g] unsalted butter, at room temperature

4 cups [500 g] confectioners' sugar

1 Tbsp vanilla extract

Pinch of salt

In a stand mixer with the paddle attachment, beat together the cream cheese and butter on medium-high speed until light in color, 3 to 5 minutes. With the mixer on low speed, slowly add the confectioners' sugar, 1 cup [125 g] at a time, until incorporated, stopping midway to scrape the sides of the bowl with a rubber spatula. Add the vanilla and salt and beat on medium-low speed until completely smooth. Use immediately or keep refrigerated in a tightly sealed container for up to 1 month; whip again before using.

VARIATION Double Chocolate Pound Cake with Chocolate Glaze

For a delicate, salty-sweet chocolate flavor, follow Mrs. Rodman's Cream Cheese Pound Cake recipe (page 239), but substitute 1 cup [125 g] of cocoa for 1 cup [125 g] of the flour. Bake the cake in a greased, floured Bundt pan.

While the cake is cooling, mix up a chocolate glaze: In a medium mixing bowl, sift together 1½ cups [180 g] of confectioners' sugar and 4 Tbsp [20 g] of cocoa powder, then add ¼ tsp of salt. Slowly whisk in 2 Tbsp of milk and 2 tsp of vanilla, a little at a time, and stir until smooth. Once the cake is cool, but while it is still on the cooling rack, drizzle the glaze over the top, letting it drip down the sides. Let sit for 10 to 15 minutes to set, then enjoy. It's one of those desserts you can't stop eating after you take that first bite. Consider yourself warned.

240

Mom's Carrot Cake

10 TO 12 SERVINGS

Carrot cake is my absolute favorite. I love the hints of spice and the depth of flavor the carrots bring out. The year I really got into baking, I wanted to make my mom's birthday cake, and when I asked her what she wanted, she surprised me by asking for carrot cake. I couldn't even think of a time she'd ever eaten it, and I'd certainly never seen her bake one. So I called her Bible study friend who always brought the best baked goods and asked her if she'd share her recipe. She gave me a few tips and pointers, and thankfully, it turned out to be a delicious cake!

I love this recipe because it always delivers a moist, well-balanced cake. I like to make it in three layers with cream cheese frosting in between and a thin, almost naked style layer of frosting around the sides.

★ NOTE ★

Prepare your cake pan with care—generously grease and line the pan for layer cakes and loaves or grease and flour for Bundts and other cake molds. Let baked cakes cool for 10 minutes but no more or they will become damp and stick to the pan. To release the cake, tap the pan firmly a few times and shake it gently to help loosen it. Set a cooling rack on top of the cake and, holding the two together, invert them so the cake can drop onto the rack. Lift away the pan and let the cake continue to cool on the rack.

2 cups [250 g] all-purpose flour

2 tsp baking soda

1 tsp cinnamon

1 tsp nutmeg

1 tsp salt

2 cups [400 g] sugar

4 eggs

1 cup [240 ml] canola oil, plus more for greasing the pans

1 tsp vanilla extract

2½ cups [225 g] grated carrots

Cream Cheese Frosting (page 240)

1 cup [100 g] chopped pecans, toasted

Preheat the oven to 325°F [165°C]. Grease and line three 8 in [20 cm] round cake pans.

In a medium mixing bowl, combine the flour, baking soda, cinnamon, nutmeg, and salt and set aside. In a stand mixer with the paddle attachment, mix together the sugar, eggs, oil, and vanilla on medium-low speed until just incorporated. With the mixer on low speed, add the flour mixture in three batches. Stop after each to scrape the sides of the bowl with a rubber spatula. Mix until combined. Remove the paddle and bowl from the mixer stand; fold in the carrots with a rubber spatula.

Evenly divide the batter between the prepared pans. Bake for 30 to 40 minutes, or until the tops are golden and a toothpick comes out clean. While the cake is cooling, prepare the Cream Cheese Frosting. Follow the basic frosting techniques for layer cake (see page 240) and press the pecans onto the sides of the cake.

Stairway Red Velvet Cake

10 TO 12 SERVINGS

Feeling burned out from New York and the Michelin kitchen lifestyle, I decided to return to my hometown of Dothan, temporarily, to recharge and make some money doing what I knew I did best—catering. My mom spread the word that I'd be back and ready to work for the holidays, and I arrived in November to a calendar booked with events.

I spent all of November and December baking and catering holiday events out of my parents' kitchen. I enlisted friends, family, and anyone I knew to help. My mom and her best friend were my resident dishwashers, and my two sisters were my only "event employees." By Christmas, I had weddings booked for spring, and I was renovating a permanent space, with no plans to leave Dothan. In the last holiday week, I baked and iced over sixty red velvet cakes in two days, lining them all the way up my parents' staircase, carefully stacking the crisp white boxes in a jigsaw puzzle of confections. Looking back, I see those stacked cakes as the steps of my future in Dothan. Each cake represented a loyal customer and added up to a community eager for more and ready to support me. I'm so thankful for my community's welcoming, encouraging spirit that kept me here in those early days, working and moving forward.

1 cup [240 ml] buttermilk

2 Tbsp red food coloring

2½ cups [315 g] all-purpose flour

1 Tbsp baking soda

1 Tbsp baking powder

1 tsp cocoa powder

½ tsp salt

1½ cups [300 g] sugar

2 eggs

1½ cups [360 ml] canola oil

1 tsp vanilla extract

1 tsp white vinegar

Cream Cheese Frosting (page 240)

1 cup [100 g] chopped pecans, toasted

Preheat the oven to 350°F [175°C]. Grease and line three 8 in [20 cm] round cake pans with parchment paper. Combine the buttermilk and red food coloring in a measuring cup and set aside.

In a medium mixing bowl, combine the flour, baking soda, baking powder, cocoa, and salt and set aside. In a stand mixer with the paddle attachment, mix together the sugar, eggs, oil, vanilla, and vinegar on medium-low speed until incorporated. With the mixer still on medium-low speed, alternately add the flour mixture and the buttermilk mixture until incorporated, stopping midway to scrape the sides with a rubber spatula.

Evenly divide the batter between the prepared pans. Bake for 30 to 40 minutes, or until a toothpick comes out clean. While the cake is cooling, prepare the Cream Cheese Frosting. Follow the frosting techniques for layer cakes (see page 240) and press the pecans onto the sides of the cake.

Acknowledgments

To my husband, Deavours. When we first started dating, I was in my early twenties, with a brand new catering business. You had no idea what you were in for, but you have managed to support me wholeheartedly with each new venture. Thank you for igniting the fire in my soul, for always encouraging me to go bigger, and for never extinguishing the flames. You are the ultimate teammate and partner, and your steadfast loyalty is the backbone of my success.

To my children, Monroe and June. I hope you are always proud of where you come from and always know you have a soft place to land. My goal is to hold you both close, but never hold you back. I hope I succeed in this over everything else in my life. Y'all inspire me to be my best.

To my mom, who has endured more vent sessions than any woman should. You've spent your entire life showing us that hard work pays off. Your dedication to family is bar none, and your boundless optimism is inspirational. Thank you for everything you do, all of the time. Your endless support is the reason I was even able to write this book.

To my dad, who taught me to always leave things better than I found them. You are a big giver from humble beginnings and a constant reminder to never, ever quit and to always do more for others.

To my siblings, to whom I give all the credit for not having an ego. Thank you for being the most honest, zero-gray-area people in my life. I value your clarity. Thank you each for assuming the roles of manager, social media expert, counselor, sous-chef, dishwasher, stylist, nanny, bodyguard, and basically anything I've needed y'all to be through this journey. I am the most annoying sister, and I am wholly aware. I appreciate and love each of you.

To my savior, Juanita, who literally keeps our home a safe haven. Your faith, advice, and life lessons have been a constant in my life since I was one year old, and it's one of my biggest joys and comforts to watch you teach my children. We love and appreciate you more than you will ever know and truly do not know what we'd do without you.

To my female friends, who each occupy a unique place in my heart. Your therapeutic cocktail hours, playdates, porch conversations, and suppers are great blessings in my life. Our friendships are the reason my life feels so full. I can't think you enough for being sure I am never bored, never cocky, and always loved. You are each so important to me. It is rare to be surrounded by women who have witnessed my huge life events and encouraged me with every step. I am grateful for the way we lift each other up, without any jealousy or ill-will. I am the luckiest to have each of you in my life.

To my KBC team, who protect my first and biggest dream. I would not be where I am or have accomplished what I have without the strong people constantly protecting my house. I am grateful daily for a team that works behind the scenes, together, to make a little family I never expected and am so blessed to have. I am most proud of the diverse team we have at KBC, who teach and inspire me daily. Thank y'all for making my dreams possible.

To my agent, Cameron, who continues to be my lighthouse in this crazy journey. You have confidently guided me through this new life. Thank you for believing

in me and opening doors I never new existed. I don't know where I'd be without your guidance and am thankful I don't have to!

To my editor, Deanne, and to the rest of the team at Chronicle Books, who somehow managed to capture my exact thoughts in a book without ever meeting me. You have taken a book that was a dream and turned it into a reality. My deepest gratitude to you for helping bring my book to life

To my literary agents, Lori and Bridget, who took a chance on me. I'm still not entirely sure why you did, but boy am I glad for it. Thank y'all for believing in this book before I did.

To Emily, the ultimate listener, transcriber, and protector of my story. I am forever grateful to you for taking such a keen and thoughtful interest in my stories and helping bring them to life. You were the first person to seriously suggest I write a book, and you connected me to the people who made it happen. Thank you, thank you, from the bottom of my heart.

Index

251